Contents

The following have generously given permission to reprint borrowed material:

Page 46: The letter from Wendy Savage was originally published in *Mathematics Teaching*, number 94 (March 1981). Used with the permission of the author.

Pages 61–62: The letter from Matt Barker was originally published in "NCTM Standards for School Mathematics: Visions for Implementation," by F. Joe Crosswhite, John Dossey, and Shirley Frye (*Mathematics Teacher*, volume 82, number 8 [November 1989]). Used with permission.

Page 78: Figure 7–1 is from *Assessment Alternatives in Mathematics* by Jean Kerr Stenmark. Copyright 1989, University of California, Lawrence Hall of Science, Berkeley, California. Used with permission.

Preface

Everyone can learn mathematics. The mathematics education reform movement suggests that this should be true, and some math teachers and mathematicians believe that it *is* true. For many years, mathematics teaching was based on the opposite premise. Not only did we assume that not everyone was capable, that "either you get it or you don't," but we also seemed to expect that only a small percentage of the student population would succeed in mastering the concepts and techniques of this demanding discipline. And experience proved us right. While American students did learn to do basic calculations, they demonstrated consistently that they were unable to solve multistep word problems. The traditional mathematics program in this country—eight or nine years of arithmetic followed by two or three years of algebra and a year of geometry—produced only a small number of students willing or able to continue on to college-level work in calculus, statistics, or other higher-level courses.

Successful or not, all students defined mathematics rather narrowly. They saw it as a collection of rules, facts, numbers, symbols, formulas, and most important, right answers. Learning mathematics required memorizing, listening passively, and following procedures. Most students never came to see that mathematics is a way of making sense of the world. For female and minority students the picture was even more dismal. Few girls or students of color enrolled in upper-level high school courses. Though the single best indicator of access to college was completion of basic algebra, in many parts of the country students finished high school without enrolling in a single algebra course.

In 1985, one of every five students in American schools was African American, Latino, or Asian. By the year 2010, the ratio will be one in three. In the middle of the twentieth century, women represented less than thirty percent of the work force. At the beginning of the twenty-first century, they will comprise fifty percent. These demographic changes present a special challenge to mathematics education. In an information-oriented world, where analytic skills will be necessary at every level of the workplace, mathematical skills are increasingly important. Few students are preparing adequately for that world.

Every year half the students enrolled in ninth-grade mathematics courses will not take tenth-grade math, and in each succeeding year the number is cut in half again. In 1990, U. S. institutions awarded 933 doctorates in the mathematical sciences, an increase of three percent over the previous year. Only 401 U. S. citizens received those degrees, however—forty-three percent of the total. Eighty-seven of those were awarded to women; four to African Americans. Who will teach the next generation of mathematicians, scientists, and teachers?

No country can afford to ignore one third of its students or one-half of its work force and expect to maintain its scientific and technological foundation. Reform studies and reports call for restructuring the mathematics curriculum in order to meet the needs of the twenty-first century.

For example, *Reshaping School Mathematics* (1990), the framework for curricular revision by the Mathematical Sciences Education Board, states that "most students receive little of lasting value from the final mathematics course they study" (5). It points out that many of those who drop out strongly dislike the subject. Calling for a change in the public philosophy of school mathematics in order to effect reform, *Reshaping School Mathematics* insists that "to know mathematics is to investigate and express relationships among patterns" (12). It calls for mathematics teaching that reflects an active, constructive view of learning.

Writing can provide opportunities for students to construct their own knowledge of mathematics. The student work that appears in this volume shows learners interpreting unfamiliar texts, constructing arguments, struggling to understand complex systems, and developing new approaches to problems. The students pose questions and compose alternative responses to those questions. Writing has given them a chance to practice inferring, communicating, symbolizing, organizing, interpreting, linking, explaining, planning, reflecting, and acting. Writing helps students make sense of mathematics. Mathematics helps students make sense of the world.

Acknowledgments

Every book is the work of many hands. This book exists because a lot of people encouraged me to finish what I'd started. I am grateful for the support of my students and colleagues at Germantown Friends School, especially members of the math department who shared their insights and the work of their students with me. Among the many students who wrote about math, Alexa Klein, John Leibovitz, Sarah Dry, Suji Meswani, Meghan Barber, Paige Levin, Tim Jucovy, Jenny Lytle, Harry Goodheart, Becky Hutcheson, Ian Childs, Noah Yaffe, Ben Cooper, David Goldstein, Sydney Poor, Derrick Robinson, Evan Sandman, Sarah Lytle, Abby Kay, Hanna Kelly, John Ashcom, Aliza Dichter, Rebecca Ewing, Elizabeth Arenson, Andrew Goldberg, Matthew Vaughan, Sam Lynch, Sophie Bryan, Eben Goodale, Jeff Zemsky, David Treat, Dustin Tracy, John Witt, Nick Fleisher, and Will Ruthrauff were kind enough to allow me to use their writing in this volume. (In order to protect the privacy of the students, the names used in the text are, in most instances, pseudonyms.)

My colleagues at the Woodrow Wilson National Fellowship Foundation, the first Functions Team—JoAnn Lutz, Lew Romagnano, and Tom Seidenberg—listened to every version of every talk I gave on writing and math, and helped me make them better. Carolyn Wilson and Henry Pollak encouraged me to speak up about my work, and gave me opportunities to do so.

Esther Cristol, Susan Lytle, Pat Macpherson, and Liz Wilson are among the many friends and colleagues who listened as I struggled with making sense of writing and mathematics teaching. My assistant at Germantown Friends School, Margaret King, put all my books and papers in order. Bob Boynton and Toby Gordon at Heinemann Educational Books put up with my procrastination. They also put me in touch with readers and editors who set everything straight.

My husband, Ed Jakmauh, and my children Rachel Countryman and Matthew Countryman, believed in the book from the start, and they endured its long gestation with good cheer. To all those named here, and to those I have forgotten to name, my heartfelt thanks.

My father, William Cannady, was my first teacher. Over many years he shared with me his love of mathematics, his interest in writing, his sense of humor, and his enthusiasm for learning. Last July, waiting in an emergency room for admission to the hospital during his last bout with leukemia, he looked at the first chapter of *Writing to Learn Mathematics*. "All parables are symmetrical and have vertexes," he read out loud, laughing. "There's some truth to that." This book is dedicated to the memory of my father, whose stories were both shapely and pointed, and who made me love teaching and learning.

One

Writing to Learn

PARABLES

A standard parable is $y = x^2$ *which looks like this* ⊍. *It keeps getting wider the farther you go up. All parables are symmetrical and have vertexes. If you add a number like* $y = x^2 + 3$ *the parable will move up on the graph. The opposite happens when you subtract a number. To make the graph skinnier multiply by a positive number,* $10x^2$ *or to make the parable wider multiply by a fraction* $1/4x^2$. *If you want to move a graph sideways try* $y = x^2 - 2x$. *That will move the graph to the left and down one. If* $y = x^2 + 2x$ *the graph will move to the right and down one. If* $y = {}^-x^2$ *the graph will turn upside down like this* ⋔ . *Parables are interesting figures.*

—A seventh grader

Unless I am badly mistaken, the writing above is not about parables. Nor is it about teaching the difference between parables and parabolas (although this seventh grader could profit from such a lesson). This writing sample demonstrates the connections between writing and thinking and learning mathematics, which also happens to be the subject of this book.

For years, I have asked my students (in grades seven through twelve) to write, read, and talk about what they are learning in math class. I want them to make sense of arithmetic, algebra, geometry, and calculus by putting into their own words the ideas and methods they are exploring. In little essays, like the one on parabolas, they record what they find.

1

Teaching and Learning Mathematics

The rules and procedures of school mathematics make little sense to many students. They memorize examples, they follow instructions, they do their homework, and they take tests, but they cannot say what their answers mean. Even the successful ones claim "I can do it, but I can't explain it." A student who says "page 73" when asked to describe what she is doing in algebra class is telling the truth: she is proceeding through the text, but she is not constructing for herself the mathematics she is trying to learn.

Knowing mathematics is doing mathematics. We need to create situations where students can be active, creative, and responsive to the physical world. I believe that to learn mathematics students must construct it for themselves. They can only do that by exploring, justifying, representing, discussing, using, describing, investigating, predicting, in short by being active in the world. Writing is an ideal activity for such processes.

A student complains, "Why do we have to write? This isn't English class; this is math." Many teachers and students resist the idea that writing belongs in math classrooms. Indeed some math teachers, like their strongest students, preferred mathematics because they imagined that it did not require much writing. Once in the classroom, however, these teachers soon realized that the practice of teaching requires making lists, notes, outlines, and plans, writing reports and comments. In addition, many math teachers agree that the way we really learn content—the arithmetic, algebra, geometry, and calculus that we teach—is by preparing lessons. Then we record our own struggle to explain the material to our students.

When students challenge me to show what writing has to do with math, I reply, "This *is* math. You know, it's fine to get the right answer, but what good is that answer if you can't explain it to anyone?" I tell them that the mathematician Henry Pollak lists the ability to communicate with others as one of the requirements for a good research mathematician. The productive use of language is a skill that all students should practice in all disciplines; reading, writing, and speaking belong in every classroom, even math classrooms.

Hence, over the years my students have recorded their work. They write about finding the slope of a line, about using the Pythagorean theorem; they describe how many squares there are on a checkerboard, how many handshakes are possible among a group of twenty people; they explain derivatives and integrals and fractions and integers.

My students write in a variety of genres. They write in journals:

> *Math has gotten totally confusing. I have hated trig functions and logs and stuff from day one—and now to combine them with calculus. It's too much! I don't think calculus is my thing. I can't figure out if I'm really confused and incapable of understanding or just lazy (but then laziness would keep me from understanding so it would be both).*

They freewrite:

> *Algebra is math with a bunch of letters that stand for numbers. They are mystery letters. When you finish the problem the letters usually turn to numbers.*
>
> —James

> *Algebra is a form of math involving variables. You learn it in 8th grade.*
>
> —Mike

> *I think algebra is very hard and confusing. It builds on itself. What may seem easy grows till it becomes very hard.*
>
> —Lisa

They write in learning logs:

POSITIVES AND NEGATIVES

> *In class we have been using $+$ and $-$. They are very hard to understand (especially subtraction of $+$ and $-$). When you are adding the same signs together $^+6 + {}^+8 = {}^+14$ it is easy, you just do normal adding keeping the signs the same. If, however, the signs are different, $^-4 + {}^+6 + {}^+2$, you just*

subtract and the higher number's sign dominates. I'm very clear on adding. On subtracting I'm not so good although I am clear on how to do it. When you are subtracting two of the same signs $^+10 - {}^+6 = {}^+4$ all you do is subtract. When the signs are different $^-6 - {}^+2 = {}^-8$ it is just adding and the higher number's sign dominates. But a hard one to solve is when the signs are different and the first digit is less than the second $(^+4 - {}^-7 = {}^+11)$ the first digit's sign will be the sign in the answer then you just add. When the digits are the same signs but the number in front is smaller $(^-3 - {}^-7 = {}^+4)$ you just subtract but you take the sign that is opposite from the problem's signs—for example if the problem's signs are − the answer sign will be +. I don't understand why but I know how to do it.

—Gary

They write math autobiographies:

To begin with, I love math! I have always loved math, since 1st grade, and I will keep on loving math until I die. It started in first grade when I got my first arithmetic book. I worked very hard that year and by the end of the year I knew my times tables. In second grade I learned short division on my own in my spare time, while in school I started mental math. I was good at that. By the time third grade started, I was well into division and I could do a little bit of long division, too, which I perfected as the year went by. The next two years I learned things like decimals, percents etc. which I had already done in fourth grade. At the end of sixth grade my parents and I made a big decision: I went 7-2 and did seventh and eighth grade in one year. The math program in 7-2 was excellent! I did Algebra I during that year and I loved it.

I'm afraid of math. I always have been. Anytime anybody works on math with me, whether it is a friend, student, teacher, or family member, I freeze up. It's like all the math I have ever learned in my whole life has left my stream of consciousness. It's only after a long time of going over a problem that I can do it confidently and easily. I have been told my instincts are good, however, I'm always afraid to go with my first answer cause I think it will be wrong. I remember one time in 10th grade, the teacher asked the class to find an easy, logical way to go about doing this problem. Nobody could seem to find a good way. After about 10 minutes I volunteered my solution and he liked it. In fact, the whole class thought it was a good method. I felt very proud.

They write about math problems:

Our problem was to find a number with 13 factors. This is how our math class went about it:

To find this number our highly intelligible minds* knew a few things if we were to find this number. First, the number had to be a perfect square, the number would also have an odd number of factors. Second, the number's square had to be prime. Before we figured these clues out, we were randomly picking numbers from the top of our heads.

We looked at many numbers before we realized that if we doubled numbers (starting with the number one) it formed a steady pattern counting by ones. We kept doubling numbers and finding the number of factors until we reached the number that had 13 factors, which is. . . . .

4096!!!   **Just joking!*

—Jenny

They write formal papers:

There are many stereotypes about mathematics: children do not like it, boys are better at it and so on. Many of these stereotypes do not hold true in the classroom. The goal of this project was to see if there is a correlation between age or sex or the child's attitude toward math and how well first grade students were able to transfer mathematical knowledge of three digit addition and subtraction of money.

A group of twenty-two first grade students were given a questionnaire which provided the data of this project. The questionnaire asked if the children liked math, if they found math hard or easy. The students had completed surveys like

*this one in the past and were accustomed to the format.
They were also uninhibited to tell their true feelings. The
survey then had ten problems of addition and subtraction
of money (dollars and cents.) The children have been doing
three digit addition and subtraction for months using only
numbers without the dollar signs and the decimal point.
Their teacher expressed her confidence that all of the children could score 90% or higher on a simple test of addition
or subtraction problems. When the signs were added, however, only twelve children were able to score a 90% or higher.*

They even write test questions:

- *Graph f° g when f(x) = |x| and g(x) = x² − 4.*
- *Write a brief essay on how the graph of f° g is different from
  the graph of x² − 4. How do the domain and range differ?*

In whatever genre, writing can motivate and enhance
the learning that takes place when students confront the concepts and procedures of mathematics. Listen to the voice of
the eleventh grader who wrote this:

*I'm beginning to feel very comfortable on the computer.
Before, I had the ability to plot a graph, but now I can
manipulate the different points and view them as an index,
a sort of enlarged table of values. Working with that I can
find zeros, turning points, etc. I wonder how to do the
slopes of curves. The difference between two points changes
when looking at different parts of the curve. I wonder if it is
in some way related to the differences between arithmetic
and squared series.*

$$1 \quad 3 \quad 5 \quad 7 \quad 9 \quad 11$$
$$2 \quad 2 \quad 2 \quad 2 \quad 2$$

$$1 \quad 4 \quad 9 \quad 16 \quad 25 \quad 36$$
$$3 \quad 5 \quad 7 \quad 9 \quad 11$$
$$2 \quad 2 \quad 2 \quad 2$$

*The differences (changes in Y) must have something to do
with the slope of a parabola.*

Listen again:

- Writing helps students become aware of what they know and do not know, can and cannot do: "I'm beginning to feel comfortable on the computer. . . . "
- When students write they connect their prior knowledge with what they are studying: "Before I had the ability to plot a graph, but now I can manipulate. . . . "
- They summarize their knowledge and give teachers insights into their understanding: ". . . I can find zeros, turning points, etc."
- They raise questions about new ideas: "I wonder how to do the slopes of curves."
- They reflect on what they know: "The difference between two points changes. . . . "
- They construct mathematics for themselves: "The differences must have something to do with the slope. . . . "

When students use language to find out what they think about mathematics, the result is often surprising. "The very fact that [the teacher] assigned writing was enough to make me start thinking," one student said of his calculus class. "We all thought this writing was ridiculous at first, but I've come to see it as the most important thing we did all year."

The connection between writing and mathematics became obvious and important to this student because of the writing *and the mathematics* that he did that year. Had he been taught mathematics as it has traditionally been taught, writing would not have made much sense. The use of writing in mathematics class, as described in this book, presupposes a different view of mathematics and mathematics instruction. In this view, mathematics is a way of thinking about the world. To understand what mathematics is we need to look at what mathematicians do, for this is a human endeavor, a thinking process the results of which come from the work of human minds.

Unfortunately, school mathematics gives our students the impression that mathematics is a dead subject, that all of its truths were discovered before 1700, when indeed considerably more mathematics has been developed and published since 1945 than in all the years of human history before that time. Little of that knowledge appears in the elementary and secondary curriculums, both of which continue to emphasize paper and pencil manipulation of symbols. An eighth grader who wrote that "Math to me shouldn't have to be anything more than $+$, $-$, $\times$, $\div$" was speaking for a large percentage of students whose vision of the discipline has been shaped by an arithmetic-driven elementary school curriculum.

Mathematicians have described a shift in contemporary mathematics away from emphasis on number and space and toward pattern and application. The distinction between pure mathematics and applied mathematics is blurring, happily, and some of the methods that have emerged—mathematical modeling, graph theory, and data analysis, for example—are accessible to younger students. These methods provide opportunities even for students in elementary grades to do real mathematics. As the following journal entry suggests, students find the work with real data compelling:

> *The problems in section 21 are enticing, they seem so real. World population, half-lives of radioactive isotopes, all these things are so physical. The ability to develop mathematical models for all this stuff is refreshing. No more of that—but what does this have to do with real life?—stuff.*

The intelligent citizen of the twenty-first century needs to know how to analyze data, how to reason in probabilistic situations, and how to make choices. What do the statistics about air quality on the front page of my newspaper mean? How should I think about situations that have a low probability of occurring but engender high risk? For example, what does a probability of one in a thousand mean in a discussion of radioactive emissions from a nuclear weapons plant? What questions should I pose to my senator about the data presented in a report on the depletion of the ozone layer?

Students at all levels need experience in identifying the kind of answer they want in a given situation. Should it be exact, or will an approximation do? Students need to know and to understand the advantages of different methods of obtaining answers. They need to know when to guess, when to use pencil and paper, when to use a calculator, how to recognize an answer, and whether the answer makes sense. A first grader, explaining how she used a calculator to find a sum, wrote:

I added 28 + 10 − 5 and it turned out to be 33 when I pressed equals and I did the thinking.

The supermarket shopper uses estimation to be certain that the ten dollars he has in his wallet will cover the cost. At the cash register it matters whether the bill is $6.28 or $62.80. Technology, particularly calculators and computers, can allow teachers and students to function at a level higher than simple addition. While the machines perform mechanical operations the time saved can be spent inferring, organizing, interpreting, explaining, constructing, planning, and reflecting.

In 1989 the National Council of Teachers of Mathematics published *The Curriculum and Evaluation Standards for School Mathematics*, a report that reflects much of this new thinking about the need for change in the mathematics curriculum. Throughout the *Standards* three features of mathematics are emphasized:

1. Knowing mathematics is doing mathematics.
2. Technology has had enormous impact on the way that mathematics is done.
3. Mathematics is now in a "golden age of production" using new methods and addressing new questions.

Fifty-four standards covering grades K–12 present new methods and questions for teachers to use in the classroom. The standards on mathematics as communication reflect the view that "to know mathematics is to engage in a quest to understand and communicate."

The language of the *Standards* reflects that emphasis on understanding and communicating. Here are a few excerpts, first from the standards for grades K–4, which state that students should be able to "relate physical materials, pictures, and diagrams to mathematical ideas," "reflect on and clarify their thinking about mathematical ideas and situations," and "relate their everyday language to mathematical language and symbols."

In grades 5–8, students are expected to "reflect and clarify their own thinking about mathematical ideas and situations," "use the skills of reading, listening, and viewing to interpret and evaluate mathematical ideas," and "discuss mathematical ideas and make conjectures and convincing arguments."

In grades 9–12, students should learn to "reflect upon and clarify their thinking about mathematical ideas and relationships," "formulate mathematical definitions and express generalizations discovered through investigations," and "express mathematical ideas orally and in writing."

With such a clear emphasis on understanding and communicating, it shouldn't be surprising that math teachers have been turning to writing.

Most teachers know that successful learning requires reinforcement, feedback, synthesis, and action. Certain attributes of writing correspond with each of these. Writing strengthens a student's experience of a new concept. Students get immediate feedback from the words that they produce. When students write, they are integrating the work of the hand, the eye, and the brain. They fix on the page connections and relationships between what they already know and what they are meeting for the first time. When they write, students are active and engaged.

It is the activity that appeals to me. Writing gets everyone involved. In *Writing to Learn* (1988), William Zinsser examines the fear of writing and traces the potential of writing-across-the-curriculum. When Zinsser visited my eleventh-grade pre-calculus class he found students writing about trigonometry.

> Mrs. Countryman drew a triangle on the blackboard and told the class she wanted them to determine the size of its three angles. But she gave them none of the information they would need—for instance, the length of the sides.
>
> "I want you to write how you might go about solving this problem when you do get more information from me," she said. The students wrote for about five minutes.

They looked like writers—they were thinking hard and laboriously putting sentences on paper and crossing out sentences that obviously didn't express what they were thinking, perhaps because their thinking kept changing as they wrote and discovered what they really thought. They even sounded like writers; I heard the scratching out of words that is the obbligato of a writer's life.

After that some of them were asked to read what they had written. The papers were all brief journeys into logic: if I knew *this* I'd be able to find out *that;* what I need to determine is *a,* so the best method to use is probably *x* and *y*. Writing and thinking and learning had merged into one process. (165–66)

The Writing Process

Writing, of course, takes many forms. Proponents of process writing describe three broad categories of student work: expository, expressive, and personal writing.[1] Expository writing, which has structure and rules, is most common in schools. Expressive writing often takes the form of stories or poems. There is evidence that the best expository and expressive work evolves from personal writing, which is closest to inner speech and to the thinking process. This is the writing that helps us come to terms with new ideas. It takes the form of notes, letters, or journal entries, and is not governed by rules of grammar or syntax. When students learn to use language to find out what they think they become better writers and thinkers. Our students need more classroom opportunities to do informal writing, to make sense by making meaning, to create for themselves the underlying concepts of mathematics.

Writing mathematics can free students of the assumption that math is just a collection of right answers to questions posed by someone else. Writing—and this includes writing notes, lists, observations, feelings, in addition to term papers, lab reports, and essay questions—will expand the narrow view of mathematics that many students carry around in their heads, a view reflected in this journal entry:

*Math to me shouldn't have to be anything more than
+, −, ×, ÷. All of the other math is really ridiculous to
have. I think that if you would like to know how to do all
that math you should be able to learn, but if you don't want
to you shouldn't.*

—Kate (an eighth grader)

Our goals—in math and in all disciplines—are much
more ambitious than Kate's. We want students to learn to
interpret unfamiliar texts, to construct convincing arguments,
to understand complex systems, to develop new approaches to
problems, and to negotiate the resolution of those problems in
groups, to pose questions and to evaluate alternative responses
to those questions. The skills they need to reach those goals
are also the same. Students need opportunities to organize,
interpret, and explain, to construct, symbolize, and communicate, to plan, infer, and reflect. Practicing these fundamen-
tal skills will help them learn mathematics.

Two

Getting Started

Mathematics teachers who have not had students write to learn usually ask me how to start. "Won't students say 'This isn't English class' when I give them a writing assignment?" teachers ask. "How can I get them to write anything?" Of course, some students will complain, but most are surprisingly responsive to brief assignments. Five minutes at the beginning of class can be productive. You might ask students to:

- Describe what we did in class yesterday.
- Explain what went wrong on problem 3 in the test.
- Discuss the most difficult homework problem.

With more time students might:

- Explore the relative merits of two different procedures.
- Write a letter to an absent classmate about the new theorem.

Any of these tasks is enough to launch the writing portion of your course. Once students are writing they are automatically taking an active role in the classroom. Instead of waiting for the teacher, or another student, to do, explain, discuss, summarize, or evaluate, each student is engaged in the learning process.

Freewriting

Freewriting is writing rapidly for a short and fixed period of time. Toby Fulwiler, the director of the writing project at the University of Vermont, describes freewriting as a good technique for dumping ideas out quickly. I often ask students to freewrite for five minutes at the beginning of the period about anything that occurs to them, or about the subject of a new unit. This writing encourages them to let their thoughts flow freely, to raise questions, and to discover what they already know about topics in algebra or calculus. The following statements are taken from freewriting by eighth graders just starting Algebra I in the fall.

> *Algebra is math with a bunch of letters that stand for numbers. They are mystery letters. When you finish the problem the letters usually turn to numbers.*
>
> —James

> *Algebra is a form of math involving variables. You learn it in 8th grade.*
>
> —Mike

> *I think algebra is very hard and confusing. It builds on itself. What may seem easy grows till it becomes very hard.*
>
> —Lisa

Students are surprised by how easy it is to start, and some are frustrated by the rush of topics that emerge. They complain that their pens cannot keep up with their thoughts. Others need to be prodded. Often I suggest that if they cannot think of anything to write they should write the sentence "I have nothing to write" for a while until something else comes to mind. The point is to force yourself to get the page dirty, to fill the page as much as possible. Such informal writing fosters independent thinking because it reminds students that learning and thinking are active, not passive. The class begins with students not as receivers of information but as agents of their own learning.

I try to join the students while they write, at least part of the time, and occasionally I share my own journal entries with the class.

Learning Logs

Many teachers of mathematics or science courses find that having students keep an informal learning log is a good place to start. A notebook, in which students record examples and brief accounts of classroom discussions, can be expanded to incorporate more of the language of struggle that is at the core of doing mathematics. The learning log is a personal record of what is transpiring in the course. Students can be encouraged to write comments about the material, their own work, their progress, and the class in general. A five- or ten-minute session at the end of the week is a good time for students to assess their understanding of a new topic. Here is a seventh grader describing work on integers:

> *In math I know a rule for the subtraction of negative and positive numbers. If you have for example $^+6 - {}^-2$ you add the two together and the answer would be positive eight. If you had the problem $^-2 - {}^+6$ the answer would be $^-8$.*
>
> *In addition you simply take the two numbers and subtract the lesser number from the greater number: example, $^+3 + {}^-6$*

$$\begin{array}{r} ^-6 \\ + {}^+3 \\ \hline ^-3 \end{array}$$

> *You then take the sign of the larger number and apply it to your answer.*
>
> —Sam

In this entry Sam has gone to the heart of the matter—the troublesome result of subtracting a positive integer from a negative, or vice versa. He developed his rule after practicing subtraction by manipulating colored tiles representing positive and negative numbers. Notice that Sam's rule works.

Notice also that his paper suggests that the real issue for Sam is sorting out the mechanics that require him to add when subtracting and to subtract when adding.

EVERYTHING I KNOW ABOUT ADDING AND SUBTRACTING

I know that you can add easily by knowing if both the labels are positive or negative then you do regular adding like this:

$$^-2 + {}^-2 = {}^-4$$

If you're adding with a negative and a positive you take the sign that is on the first number and do regular adding and then put that sign on the number like this:

$$^-2 + {}^+4 = {}^-6$$

When doing subtracting you have to take the number that you are subtracting from and then add that many zeros like this:

$$^+8 - {}^-4 = {}^+12$$

—Suzanne

Suzanne's mistake ($^-2 + {}^+4 = {}^-6$) would simply be marked wrong on a quiz or test. Her explanation told me that she was not ready to construct a rule. Indeed, the contrast between her example and her explanation of subtraction is interesting.

Using the tiles, we represented the number zero by placing a positive and a negative together like this:

Adding zero to a number does not change its value but allows for subtraction of negative or positive numbers that seem to be missing. Suzanne was able to show that by adding four zeros to positive eight she could then subtract negative four from positive eight and get positive twelve, but, with the phrase "add that many zeros" she describes adding eight zeros. In each case, the words tell me considerably more about the student's understanding than the numbers do.

I have addition down pretty pat. The rule I have come up with is this. When I am adding two numbers that are both negative or that are both positive I keep them the same and just add, like this:

$$+3 + {}^+3 = {}^+6 \qquad \& \qquad {}^-3 + {}^-3 = {}^-6$$

When they are opposite it depends. Whichever number is higher you keep the sign the same as that. From there you just subtract the lower number from the higher number, like this:

$$+8 + {}^-4 = {}^+4 \qquad \& \qquad {}^+4 + {}^-8 = {}^-4$$

Subtraction I know pretty well but it is hard to put a rule in writing. When both numbers are positive or both are negative and you are subtracting a lower number from a higher number you keep it the same and just subtract, like this:

$$+7 - {}^+4 = {}^+3 \qquad \& \qquad {}^-7 - {}^-4 = {}^-3$$

When you are subtracting a higher number from a lower number it is different. When they are both positive or negative you change it to the other and subtract it backwards, like this:

$$+3 - {}^+8 = {}^-5 \qquad \& \qquad {}^-3 - {}^-8 = {}^+5$$

When the two signs are opposite it is also different. You keep the sign the same as it is with the first number and add the two numbers together, like this:

$$+5 - {}^-3 = {}^+8 \qquad \& \qquad {}^-3 - {}^+5 = {}^-8$$

Those are my rules for subtracting and adding positive and negative numbers.

—Cindy

Cindy offers a comprehensive summary of her knowledge. She has selected a catalog of examples—adding positives, adding negatives, adding a positive and a negative, subtracting positives or negatives with the subtrahend smaller, etc.—and, although she offers a mild disclaimer about putting the subtraction rules into words, her rules do work. "Change it to the other and subtract it backwards" is an awkward construction, but it challenges a reader to think about what is happening with subtraction.

POSITIVES AND NEGATIVES

In class we have been using + and −. They are very hard to understand (especially subtraction of + and −). When you are adding the same signs together ⁺6 + ⁺8 = ⁺14 it is easy, you just do normal adding keeping the signs the same. If, however, the signs are different, ⁻4 + ⁺6 = ⁺2, you just subtract and the higher number's sign dominates. I'm very clear on adding. On subtracting I'm not so good although I am clear on how to do it. When you are subtracting two of the same signs ⁺10 − ⁺6 = ⁺4 all you do is subtract. When the signs are different ⁻6 − ⁺2 = ⁻8 it is just adding and the higher number's sign dominates. But a hard one to solve is when the signs are different and the first digit is less than the second (⁺4 − ⁻7 = ⁺11) the first digit's sign will be the sign in the answer then you just add. When the digits are the same signs but the number in front is smaller (⁻3 − ⁻7 = ⁺4) you just subtract but you take the sign that is opposite from the problem's signs—for example if the problem's signs are − the answer sign will be +. I don't understand why but I know how to do it.

—Gary

You can almost hear Gary thinking as you read his description of what he has noticed about operations on integers. Since he indicated that addition was clear, I wrote him a note suggesting that he try changing a subtraction problem to an addition problem and using his rules for addition, for example ⁺4 − ⁻7 = ⁺4 + ⁺7 = ⁺11. Of course, he will still need to think about why my rule works, but referring back to the colored tiles might help him see a connection between addition and subtraction. For all of these seventh graders the combination of writing and working with manipulatives contributes to their understanding operations on integers, a concept that for many students never makes any sense.

Other Strategies

- Ask students to write you a short note on the back of the homework paper:

  — Was the assignment hard or easy?
  — Which problem was most difficult?
  — What did you learn that was new?
  — What do you not understand?

- When you give a reading assignment ask students to write a list of the main ideas, definitions of new terms, or description of new methods,

- Include definitions and verbal descriptions of mathematical processes on tests. For example, "Explain how to subtract one integer from another if their signs are different."

- Ask students to compare and contrast different procedures. For example, "What methods have you learned for solving systems of linear equations? What are the advantages and disadvantages of each method? Which do you prefer?"

- Use prompts or sentence stems to get them started:

  — I think calculators . . .
  — Factoring is easy if . . .
  — The trouble with math is . . .
  — I can do word problems when . . .
  — Math is like . . .
  — Prime numbers are . . .
  — Teachers usually say . . .
  — To study for a math test I usually . . .

Summary

- Informal writing tasks are particularly useful in mathematics. They require little time, but they help students become active learners.

- Freewriting, the writing that is closest to speech, can help students find out what they know, and what they do not know, about math.

- Learning logs, which can begin as simple extensions of the students' notebooks, serve as personal records of the experience of doing mathematics.
- Commenting on an assignment, writing a definition, comparing procedures, or completing a sentence stem are all examples of writing tasks that can easily be included in any mathematics course.

Three

Autobiography

Dear Joan Countryman,

The best thing I can do in math is fractions and decimals, and the worst thing is measurement. I worked with Integers for 1 week and did all right.

—Martin, seventh grade

Everyone has a mathematics autobiography. Students bring to their classes a long history of doing math, in and out of school, and a set of ideas about the nature of mathematics and their own ability to do and understand it. Early in my teaching career I asked the students in my second-year algebra class to write a mathematics autobiography. "Tell me about your triumphs and disasters," I said. "Go back as far as you can remember. What do you like about learning math? What do you not like?"

The results were astonishing. My tenth-grade algebra students had specific, detailed memories about fractions and long division, about tests in third grade and pop quizzes in eighth, about word problems and problems with words.

Math is my favorite subject. Last year I took an Algebra I course for the year and scored a 99% on my final exam. Math has always come easy for me. Kindergarten through now math has been my best subject. One of my main problems was (and is) word problems. I just can't seem to get the work between the problem and the solution. I get the answer without doing the in-between stuff. I also am kind of silent in class, but will answer when called upon. I am good at doing things that are logical, but not if I don't understand them. I was in the top two males of our own age level in our school, and in the top 5 girls and boys.

Asking students to write a mathematics autobiography at the beginning of the school year gives them permission to talk about what they know best: themselves, what they care about, and what they know. It also helps students focus on their own learning styles and think about what works and does not work for them. In addition, writing enables many students to take more responsibility for what goes on in class, for as they write about doing mathematics they come to see themselves as central to the process of learning.

Students often associate bad feelings about mathematics with a teacher whose demands, perceived by the student as unrealistic and unreasonable, made mathematics too seem unrealistic and irrational.

To tell you the truth I have never really liked math. Even when I was little I always dreaded math time. Maybe all those numbers scare me. There have been many times when I didn't understand a certain process and the teachers failed to help me. They want me to figure it out on my own but that makes me frustrated (I get aggravated very easily!) and even more uncapable. I usually only enjoy math when it's made really fun. Otherwise I'm bored.

To start off I will tell you that math is not one of my most favorite subjects. I do not yet see how some of the things we learn will help us later on in life—for example $2x^2 + 7x + 3 = (x + 3)(2x + 1)$. I do not know whether or not my feelings will change, but for now this is how I feel. One of my most favorite things to do in math is area & perimeter. Last year we did the areas and perimeters of triangles, rectangles, squares, and squares with chunks taken out. One of my most unpopular things to do in math is working with the calculator. I found it hard to understand and therefore found it difficult to do. I found working with the compasses boring. I really liked doing percentages & decimals and working with fractions (dividing). There *is one last thing I think you should know, I really do not like tests!*

Writing about these experiences, and hearing from their classmates, encourages students to acknowledge that mathematics does engender feeling. Sharing these memories will bring laughter into the classroom. Students are often surprised to discover that others feel the way they do. They regard their triumphs differently, and offer their success stories as evidence of their own powers. Writing contributes to the movement toward an inclusive curriculum, one that invites students to see themselves as mathematicians.

To begin with, I love math! I have always loved math, since 1st grade, and I will keep on loving math until I die. It started in first grade when I got my first arithmetic book. I worked very hard that year and by the end of the year I knew my times tables. In second grade I learned short division on my own in my spare time, while in school I started mental math. I was good at that. By the time third grade started, I was well into division and I could do a little bit of long division, too, which I perfected as the year went by. The next two years I learned things like decimals, percents etc. which I had already done in fourth grade. At the end of sixth grade my parents and I made a big decision: I went 7-2 and did seventh and eighth grade in one year. The math program in 7-2 was excellent! I did Algebra I during that year and I loved it.

I like finding the answer to math problems quickly and well without a whole lot of trouble. I also like being told how to do a problem and doing it without trouble. I don't like long calculator problems and I don't like long lectures about how to do the problem, when it could be explained simply in 2 minutes. I don't ask for help a whole lot. A couple of years ago I had a lot of trouble with word problems and it was a disaster. I guess I do fine in math once I understand the concept.

I got an early start with numbers when my brother used to teach me before I started school. Since then I have had a good understanding of how they work. The only time I don't like math is when it gets boring. When you do the same thing day after day. Usually I am fairly quick at taking in new ideas and solving problems. Most years, including last year, I have gotten pretty good scores in math and some years have found it a pretty enjoyable subject. Math has always been one of my stronger points in school.

Teachers who ask their students to write their math histories early in the year report that they know considerably more about their students much earlier in the year than they did previously. Issues like confidence and self-esteem, of concern in teaching any discipline but especially significant in the mathematics classroom, are brought into the open where they can be confronted.

I'm afraid of math. I always have been. Anytime anybody works on math with me, whether it is a friend, student, teacher, or family member, I freeze up. It's like all the math I have ever learned in my whole life has left my stream of consciousness. It's only after a long time of going over a problem that I can do it confidently and easily. I have been told my instincts are good, however, I'm always afraid to go with my first answer cause I think it will be wrong. I remember one time in 10th grade, the teacher asked the class to find an easy, logical way to go about doing this problem. Nobody could seem to find a good way. After about 10 minutes I volunteered my solution and he liked it. In fact, the whole class thought it was a good method. I felt very proud.

Reading math histories also helps teachers see their students as individual learners with passions, needs, and beliefs about knowledge and themselves.

When I was in the early part of the lower school I never finished my math books during the year and I was forced to take them home over the summer. That only happened in the first three years and from fourth grade on I seemed to do all right in math. In seventh grade I did very well in my pre-algebra course. Then I had algebra in 8th grade, and it was like hitting a brick wall. I did even worse the next year in geometry and only made a slight improvement in algebra two. During eighth grade I learned to hate math with a passion. It might of had more to do with the teacher I had than it did with the subject, but the feelings linger just the same. I admit to feeling frustrated in the beginning but that feeling left quickly and was replaced by a feeling of resentment that questioned why I was learning this stuff at every turn.

Math autobiographies set the tone for yearlong conversations between my students and me about their interests, performance, and learning styles. Twenty years ago I was surprised by the candor and openness of those tenth graders who were so willing to let me know how they felt about math. Now I have come to expect the rich detail, and the honesty, that comes with these reflections, but each new voice still moves me to think carefully about my classroom practice.

Up to about fifth grade I enjoyed and was quite good at math. After that, I often became confused, and, most of all, frustrated by it. A main problem that I have in math is that I will understand some of the material very well, but when I don't catch something right away or in a short amount of time, I have a problem ever understanding it. Sometimes I get so frustrated, I think I hold myself back from learning it. This is strange, because sometimes I find things which other people have trouble with quite easy, and vice-versa. Either way, I always end up doing badly in math, and that's probably why I dislike it.

Before ninth grade, math to me was just drudgery—I struggled through, barely comprehending, uninterested and even angry when I fell behind, but unable to force myself to be so accepting of things I didn't understand. That is, until Geometry. Geometry started putting things into place for me—it gave reasons and proofs and laws. Causes led to effects—a rational science. I excelled in Geometry. Last year, however, things went downhill. We were asked to memorize, without explanation of the nagging questions "Why does this happen this way?" or "Are you sure this is always true?" It felt as though we were rushed through a lot in order to cover a lot of ground. I'd rather cover less and really understand more.

Summary

- Autobiography helps students see themselves as central to the learning process.
- Reading math autobiographies helps teachers see students as individual learners with passions, interests, concerns, needs, beliefs.
- Acknowledging feelings about mathematics contributes to the movement toward an inclusive curriculum.
- Writing autobiographies brings the disasters out into the open so that students can be freed from the anxious hiding of their feelings of inadequacy.
- Autobiographies bring laughter into the classroom, and sharing their math histories helps students see that others feel the way they do.

Four

Journals

A few years ago I started asking my students to keep mathematics journals in order to record their experience of learning mathematics. I tell them that a journal is a chart of their journey through the course and a way for them to keep track of where they are going, and where they have been, as they struggle with the stuff of mathematics. Now, of course, my students expect that they will be asked to write about mathematics and about themselves learning mathematics, but students in those first classes approached the task with healthy skepticism. What did writing have to do with math?

I told them that one good way to clarify their thinking was to keep a running account of their work. A journal is a good place for freewriting. I encouraged them to suspend judgment in the journal and to feel free to ask questions, to experiment, to make statements about what they did and did not understand. They needed help, at first, to learn to write without censoring their thoughts. They needed to feel confident that no one else would censure or criticize what they had written. So, I told them to leave their "personal editors" (the critical voice in their own heads) at the door. I assured them that while I did care about grammar, spelling, and punctuation, nevertheless on these "first draft" entries I would neither evaluate nor criticize their writing. Corrections could come later, if they chose to edit an entry themselves. Otherwise, anything they were willing to let me read was acceptable.

Ellen, a twelfth-grade calculus student, began a long conversation about her approach to learning that confirmed my sense of her growing confidence in her own abilities.

I guess I should say something about my style—in a word it's wordy. Actually I just approach things the roundabout way. . . . I enjoy writing. I also enjoy math. Perhaps I enjoy it because we are usually presented with solvable problems—or perhaps just because it is so "neat." Everything with ∫ and derivatives is somehow connected in what seems to be a fluke but I suppose is really the closest to perfection in a natural thing. (Although one could argue its invention, calculus must have existed in concept—some universal infinite one no doubt.) Maybe I just feel so positive about math right now because I am at a point where everything seems clear.

Roger, a very quiet student in the same class, used the journal to explore his ideas about the difference between the mechanics of math and the concepts.

I think that when it comes to math I am much more interested in concepts than actual numerical equations. Most people complain about how math applies to real life, but that part doesn't bother me. In its truest form, math has nothing to do with reality. None of it actually exists. What is important is how the unreal concepts can be applied to real life situations. There is little excitement in plugging in numbers, but when math is philosophical, related to physics, chemistry or biology, or even sexual, is when it is most exciting. Math that can be done on a computer should be done in a computer which can do it faster and more accurately. I find the math that cannot be programmed to be much more important.

Reading math journal entries tells me considerably more about what students grasp and do not understand, like and dislike, care about and reject as they study mathematics than any formal or traditional math assignments. I find myself more aware of what students know, and how they come to construct that knowledge. Robin, an eleventh grader who claimed to prefer philosophy to mathematics, wrote:

What is math class? My topic for today is the definition of math class and definition itself, for that matter. Actually, I was thinking about it today in meeting [for worship] for some reason. It just struck me that while I'm sitting behind my desk in the [classroom] building, for that 40 minutes, I sit and think about and try to define things that have no practical meaning to me (numbers) and the more I learn, the less I think what I'm doing is important. I mean, how many right triangles am I going to meet. I mean if I'm not an architect or engineer. I'm not going to be either. I'm going to be a politician. Is it going to help my political career that I know by heart the cosine of 45°?

So, I was thinking again about this idea of trying to understand concepts I only deal with 40 minutes a day (not including weekends). For some reason, I think that it has a lot to do with personality. I love to think about philosophy—why we exist, what particular philosophers think, why there is/isn't a heaven or should/shouldn't be morals, etc. But although I realize Pythagoras is a philosopher, I never understood him and felt satisfied just thinking— well this looney tune thought the number 1 was a person and defined the world by using numbers. That I didn't understand why he wanted to do this (unless it's because numbers are pretty organizable and follow themselves consecutively and have order) and how he could try to make these abstracts a reality didn't bother me because I don't understand that much about math either. For me, math is just this other world, like on TV or in a movie or something. It's interesting to look at (40 minutes a day) but it just doesn't fit with my real world.

I ask my students to use the journal to help them think about themselves learning math; to raise and respond to questions that originate in class discussions, to make connections between their own experiences and the course, to reflect on anything they consider relevant, and to carry on a conversation with me, their teacher.

Sometimes that conversation is formalized in a dialogue journal, which is a recorded conversation between teacher and student about the nature of mathematics and the individual student's progress through the course. Here is an example of one such conversation:

STUDENT: *My questions are related to the last test. I do not understand why the derivative of* ln(x/2) *does not equal* 1/x − 1/2. *I will probably be able to figure that out on my own eventually.*

JC: *Well, if* $y = \ln(x/2)$ *you can think of the derivative in two ways:* $y = \ln u$ *(with* $u = x/2$*), or* $y = \ln x − \ln 2$ *(using the properties of logs).* ln 2 *is a constant so its derivative is 0. You can take it from there.*

Not all students respond with enthusiasm to the journal assignments. "I really fail to see the point," one wrote. "Journals are so English." Nevertheless, the informal mode appeals to many, and I was surprised to find how easily students were willing to share with me their feelings, opinions, and preoccupations. Answering the journal entries was not difficult. Sometimes a word or a phrase would do; at other times I wrote a long note, posed a set of questions, or suggested an alternative view.

In an essay for teachers on the classroom use of journals, Toby Fulwiler (1987) provides a list of features to look for when responding to and assessing the content of student journals. Many of the elements in the list are especially helpful to math and science teachers who are not accustomed to reading and evaluating student writing.

Fulwiler divides the characteristics into three categories: language features, cognitive activities, and document features. Although the language is generally informal, personal, and emotional, evidence of remarkable thinking strategies is often present in journals. The form, structure, and nature of the journal can provide insight into its quality as a teaching and learning tool. Some examples of student writing will illustrate these features.

Language

Common features of journal entries include the personal voice, a conversational tone, and unexplained references.

> *After several days of being lost in class I finally sat down tonight and did #3 all the way through. It was so easy I got worried. Where were the parabolic and hyperbolic curves I saw Sarah and Evan drawing? This is what we are doing in physics now so I can get it. Now the only thing that confuses me is why I was confused before.*

Punctuation is often informal, the tone is experimental and playful (see Figure 4–1). Also, students have strong feelings about mathematics, so in a journal you can expect to find superlatives, passion, and bias.

> *I don't know how I feel about the test tomorrow. If the test is like the chapter review than it should be okay. That is if I did the Review right. I am kind of nervous about the questions like "in what quadrant is angle R when the cosine is negative." I hate those problems.*

> *I'm so confused in math I feel like I did in 8th grade—so lost I don't even know how to start to try to understand! I also simply don't have the drive. I don't care. I hate logs. I hate trig and I don't understand what e is the natural log of and what good it does us. It actually looks like it's all pretty simple but some small but key element that I need to learn it is missing.*

Although I tell my students that they may write anything in their journals as long as they are willing to let me read it, most of what they write has something to do with math and learning math. But occasional glimpses into adolescent fancy show up as well.

> *I don't have anything to write about. It's raining and yucky outside. We were discussing Vietnam in History class. I'm tired because I only had 4 hours of sleep last night + the night before. I can't stop thinking about the prom! It should be fun. Boredom. It's an art form! I wonder how many*

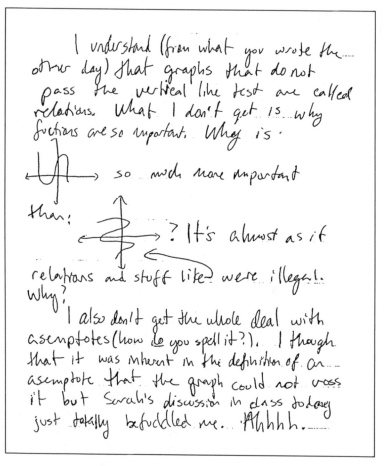

I understand (from what you wrote the other day) that graphs that do not pass the vertical line test are called relations. What I don't get is why functions are so important. Why is

so much more important than:

? It's almost as if relations and stuff like were illegal. Why?

I also don't get the whole deal with asemptotes (how do you spell it?). I thought that it was inherent in the definition of an asemptote that the graph could not cross it but Sarah's discussion in class today just totally befuddled me. Ahhhh.

Figure 4–1. An entry in Anna's journal

*positions I can be bored in in this desk. Hmmmmmm.
Human beings have no right to be bored ever. There are
only a couple bazillion things you can possibly think about.
It's just a matter of choosing one. But I'm still bored.*

Cognition

Good journals give evidence of students using a wide variety
of thinking skills, again providing a teacher with considerably

more information about how students are approaching and using mathematical concepts than most formal assignments can offer. In the entries that follow you will see students observing, speculating, doubting and confirming, questioning, revising, posing and solving problems of their own composition.

The next two excerpts are taken from journals of twelfth-grade calculus students writing in the spring as they prepare for the advanced placement exam.

Why is π such a fascinating concept? Why is there that silly desire to know pi *to thousands and thousands of digits? Clearly, unless one must have extremely precise numbers* pi *to even 10 digits is more than enough. I see this fascination with exactness now in calculating "e," just as I did 2 years ago over $\sqrt{2}$. This is more than a mere fad. It is a deep interest in the useless and unnecessary. Why do certain people try to express irrational numbers as if they were rational numbers? The only answer I can figure to any of these questions is that there may be a faint hope that whatever ancient Greek said that π was irrational was wrong. Perhaps it is the allure of discovering π is actually 22/7.*

I figured out the meaning of life. Life is a three dimensional picture show and what matters is the perspective you choose to observe it through. Sometimes you should look at "the big picture"; in fact, most of the time you should. Other times you can involve minute aspects of the movie in your everyday affairs. BUT!! Don't take it too seriously because life is a comedy. 2 is a very simple number. $\sqrt{}$ is a very simple idea. But the two simple things, when mixed together, become excruciatingly complex ($\sqrt{2}$!!) Too many people think about $\sqrt{2}$ and forget about 2 or $\sqrt{}$. That's a no-no. Like calculus, another important aspect of life is not A or B but the change (Δ) from A to B (or vice versa). We change so much in life it is far better to accept its inevitability than to fight it. The hard part is accepting it when you are happy because the common assumption is that it can only be a change for the worse. If you are at the top of a mountain you can only go down, right? Wrong!! You can also jump to the top of a new and different mountain.

Here an eleventh grader writes about her first encounter with triangle trigonometry.

LAW OF COSINES

$$c^2 = a^2 + b^2 - 2ab \cos C$$

I don't understand why there aren't angles in the equation, but I guess that it's because the law of cosines enables us to use small (limiting) amounts of information in order to find out missing angles & sides. This seems similar to a quadratic formula kind of thing.

A seventh grader blends comments about learning to play lacrosse with her work in math:

Lacross started yesterday. It was really a lot of fun playing and learning new skills. The sport of lacross can be very hazardous though. People can poke the stick at you, the ball could knock you out. But, I love the feeling of running with the wind and having the ball in my stick while I'm cradling. To cradle is a very hard skill because your whole body has to move with it as well. It is also very hard to run & cradle at the same time. Nonetheless, I want to be on the A team and learn to play a good game of lacross to someday be on JV or Varsity.

Today in math we have a test on what we have learned in class during the 1st week. It is all about geoboards. It will probably be a test on finding area. I didn't really study for this, but I am familiar with it anyway.

Document Features

Students can learn to evaluate their own use of journals as a learning tool if teachers will draw attention to matters like frequency, length, source of topics, chronology, and themes. Frequent and longer entries will usually prove more useful to the student, and those who write regularly soon begin to raise their own questions (see Figure 4–2). Sometimes just drawing attention to the length of an entry by asking students to "try to fill the page" or "write more than a

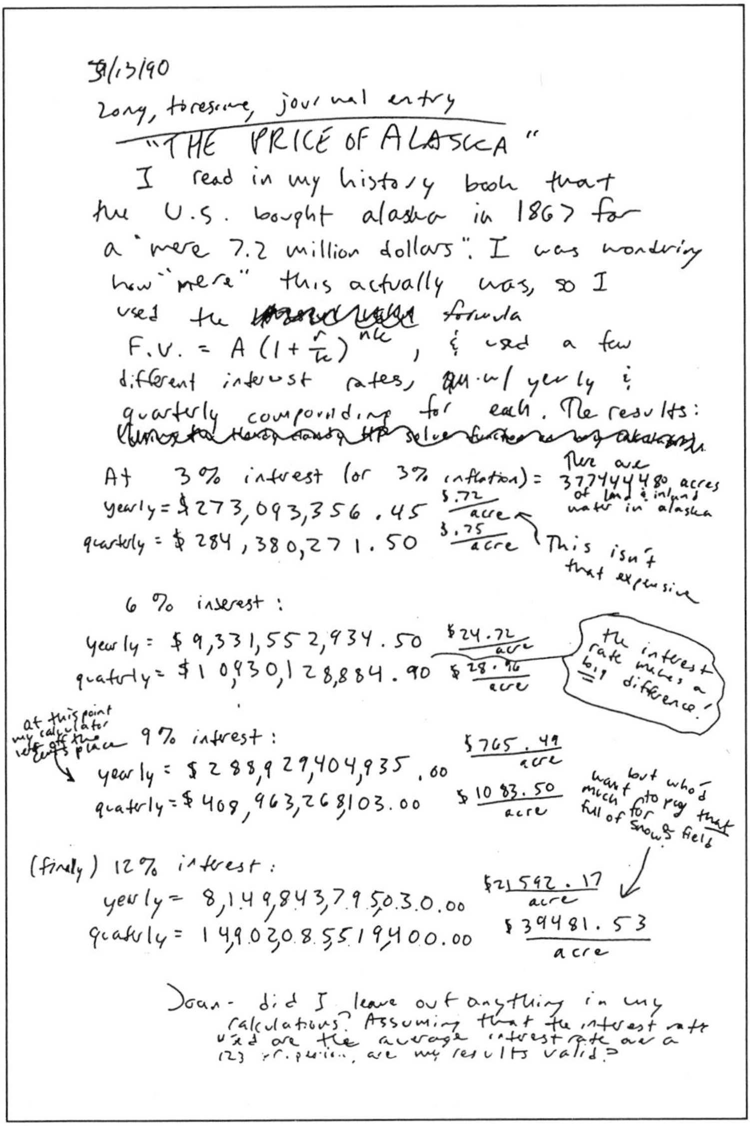

3/13/90

Long, foreseeing, journal entry

"THE PRICE OF ALASKA "

I read in my history book that
the U.S. bought alaska in 1867 for
a "mere 7.2 million dollars". I was wondering
how "mere" this actually was, so I
used the ~~compound interest~~ formula
$F.V. = A(1 + \frac{\hat{r}}{k})^{nk}$, & used a few
different interest rates, annual/yearly &
quarterly compounding for each. The results:
~~Alaska has been sold further & further...~~

At 3% interest (or 3% inflation) = 377,444,480 acres
yearly = \$ 273,093,356.45 $\frac{5.72}{acre}$ of land & inland
quarterly = \$ 284,380,271.50 $\frac{3.75}{acre}$ water in alaska
This isn't
that expensive

6% interest :
yearly = \$ 9,331,552,934.50 $\frac{\$24.72}{acre}$
quarterly = \$10,930,128,884.90 $\frac{\$28.96}{acre}$ the interest
rate makes a
big difference!

at this point
my calculator
went off place   9% interest :
yearly = \$ 288,929,404,935.60 $\frac{5765.49}{acre}$
quarterly = \$ 409,963,268,103.00 $\frac{\$1083.50}{acre}$ want but who'd
much to pay that
full of for
snow & field

(finally) 12% interest :
yearly = 8,149,843,795,030.00 $\frac{\$21,592.17}{acre}$
quarterly = 149,020,855,194,00.00 $\frac{\$39481.53}{acre}$

Joan - did I leave out anything in my
calculations? Assuming that the interest rate
used are the average interest rate over a
123 yr period, are my results valid?

Figure 4–2. "The Price of Alaska"

sentence or two" will help students make better use of language to explain what they are learning.

Journal Conversations

I started student journals for the first time one spring term. In that first year, I noticed that the journal entries recorded the extended conversations I was having with students about their thoughts, feelings, and reactions to the class. Whether brief or extended, my responses to the entries served to keep those conversations alive.

JC: *What do you think about finite volume and infinite surface area?*

STUDENT: *I thought that the apartment building in the movie "Infinite Acres" was a lot like a string. It was getting smaller and smaller until it would become one dimensional. A string (or a one dimensional line) can be thought of as having no volume as there is no depth or height, but it still has surface area. The volume is zero and the surface area infinite.*

JC: *You might want to read about the snowflake curve, which has finite area but infinite perimeter.*

Some of my comments touched on the mathematical content of an entry, others responded to questions about methods:

STUDENT: *My basic problem is understanding graphically the relations between the derivative and the limit because I have trouble putting into words what the limit means. Do I have to understand that to be able to do future assignments? . . . The rules . . . which we've been working with are easily used once memorized. . . . Although I am not able to do all of the homework problems, I feel as if I have a good grasp of the material. . . .*

JC: *The concept of limit is important but rather elusive. You are right, it is possible to learn the rules and apply them to specific exercises without understanding the underlying concepts. The problem, of course, is that it is hard to generate anything new—or learn anything on your own that way.*

A Teacher's Journal

During that first year with student journals, I decided that I, too, should keep a journal. Reading it now reminds me about the freshness that hearing student voices in this way brought to my teaching. Right away, I began to notice my students' concerns with new eyes and ears.

March 3 *The first day of writing—freewriting—was greeted with interest and enthusiasm. Some complained about notebook colors—"Can we trade?" "I hate green" etc. What surprises and pleases me is that the writing itself seems to be taken for granted.*

I have a lot invested in this—in my theory, sense, hope— that writing helps students get in touch with how they learn mathematics. In a way it is fortuitous that I decided to try journal writing in class every day just as we were getting into transcendental functions because I am already hearing cries of complaint and confusion. P. and D. this morning both said they were sure they were the only ones who didn't understand.

I wish there were more time for me to help them become comfortable with exponential and logarithmic functions. Perhaps I can think about my own dis-ease. Working on the interest problem today put me in touch with that sense of anxiety that students must feel when they see how algebra works but can't understand why.

I was surprised by the students' willingness to try the journal idea, and I was surprised by the minimum of fuss.

March 4 *Everyone dove for the journals and settled in. (If only the seventh grade would get so involved.) My questions today have to do with class management. What shall I do with tests and quizzes? Make them shorter? Not give quizzes? Actually I don't mind giving up quizzes—someone suggested that strategy for journal writing in college courses—and the next test is the annual take-home anyway. I wonder what impact the journals will have on that experience for this class?*

Competition is a big issue for this group. Though some students seem blissfully unaware (or unconcerned?) about it, others carry a lot of resentment and anger just under the surface. I don't know how to get at that issue—or whether I should. My own style is so uncompetitive that I probably should list myself in the blissful group, happily working without attending to the cutthroat behavior raging around me. Should I take a stance that is anticompetitive? Is it relief from competition that makes this group so enthusiastic about writing? ...

Writing quickly became part of the rhythm of the class, and I looked forward to reading their entries.

March 5 *A noisy start but a single word gets them started. I said that they could only have seven minutes today and the response was wild objection. "We're addicted to this now." I know that they look forward to writing and think ahead of time about what they might write.*

March 9 *The seniors take their notebooks and start writing with little or no direction. The room becomes quiet the way meeting [for worship] does—a growing stillness. I wonder what will happen with the recalcitrant ones—like K.— who prides himself in saying as little as possible. I'd like to help him see that his approach to writing is not different from his approach to calculus. Skimming the surface; dismissing what seems, to him, insignificant; blocking himself. This sort of student cannot be confronted directly. (I think of L., who was much more successful as a math student; but I did not know that he came to appreciate the writing until long after the course ended and he had graduated.)*

Some Practical Considerations

No single method of journal keeping works for every teacher or every class, and the suggestions I offer here are just that— suggestions. I find myself changing my approach with different classes and at different times during the year. Although reading and responding to students' journals usually proves to be considerably less difficult than most teachers imagine, a few practical considerations will help smooth the process.

First, and most important: Give up the idea that you, the teacher, are responsible for correcting every punctuation, spelling, or conceptual error that you find. All of us, and especially our students, carry around in our heads conceptions and misconceptions for which only we ourselves are responsible. The journal gives a teacher access to that thinking, but not license to take on the burden of fixing all of it. Students will sort most of their own misconceptions themselves, if we let them.

Second, explain to students why you are asking them to write about themselves learning mathematics. You will find that some are skeptical, but many will appreciate your interest in their work, and they will tell you so.

Third, start by having students write in class, for five minutes at the beginning or five minutes at the end of the period. You should *write with them*, and share some of your writing, so that students see that you are serious enough about the usefulness of the experience to do it yourself.

Fourth, read the early journal entries carefully and take time to respond in some way. Your comment can be brief (*Indeed! I see!*), light and encouraging in tone (*Did you try #3? I think it's easier than #4*), or a detailed answer to a specific question (*Your question about substituting* f(x) *for* x *suggests to me a need for pictures—to illustrate both your question and my answer. What if you think of* $y = x^2 - 1$ *as a variation of* $y = x^2$?).

I generally write short comments on the journal page itself. Large Post-it notes or scratch paper clipped onto the student's entry serve for longer notes. Although it is impossible for me to write a long response to every long entry I do try to write a few substantial comments to every student sometime during the year. From reading the journals over the years I have learned that most students just want an indication that I have read their comments, and as the next entry shows, for those for whom the journal takes on real significance even that is not necessary.

> *The most important thing is [what] some of the entries helped me do. It was as if I was explaining to someone else, but since/if I didn't understand, many times in the process*

of struggling to explain it to my silent audience I came to understand it. I enjoyed getting feedback from actual human beings on journal entries, but actually, it didn't much matter by then, since I'd already struggled with whatever it was. . . . In all, I really enjoyed the journal and gained a very clear understanding of a number of the topics we studied because of it.

At the beginning of the year, after we have written in class for five minutes every day for about two weeks, I give my students this one-page statement on journals. We refer to it periodically as the year progresses.

JOURNALS

You are asked to keep a journal on 8¹/₂″ × 11″ sheets of loose leaf paper. Plan to make 3–5 journal entries per week. You need not spend more than five to ten minutes writing each entry. Each week I will collect the journal entries (on Monday) and return them with comments.

The focus of your journal entries should be your learning of mathematics. What *you* do, feel, discover, invent. Within this context you may write on any topic or issue you choose, as long as you are willing to let me see it.

To stimulate your thoughts and reflections I offer the following:

1. What did you learn from a class, activity, discussion, assignment?
2. What questions do you have about the work?
3. Describe any discoveries you make about mathematics or yourself doing mathematics.
4. Describe the process you undertook to solve a problem.
5. What confused you? challenged you? What did you like? What did you not like?

A journal can be a chart of your journey through the course. As you know, I am convinced that writing can be a powerful tool for learning mathematics. It can help you develop the critical and reflective skills necessary for you to make sense of the material that we examine in this course.

There will be no quizzes in this course. Tests will be announced and there will be a midyear exam in December and a final in the spring. There will also be a term paper or project due in the spring. We'll begin work on the projects at the beginning of the second semester.

At the end of the year I ask students to look over the journal, number the pages, choose their ten or twelve favorite entries and write a table of contents, introduction, and conclusion. A fine concluding activity, this exercise helps students look back on where they have been and how far they have come in their understanding and appreciation of the discipline. The following entries from calculus and precalculus journals—a table of contents, two introductions, and a conclusion—show how students respond to this assignment.

TABLE OF CONTENTS

INTRODUCTION

This journal was supposed to serve as a place to put down questions, solve questions, and formulate new answers; to realize what we have learned, and to find out what we haven't learned and learn it. I used it to free my mind, and allow myself to concentrate on math. For me math needs all of my focus, and my journal was a place to get this focus.

Through my writing you can see so many things that have come out that would have blocked my learning calculus.

My journal let me empty my brain onto paper. Sometimes it cleared it, other times it focused it. It often brought me to realize that I completely understood material we were working on, or most of the time, just the opposite was true. Often there was just one question, or mistake I was making that was standing in the way of my comprehension of the material, and my journal often helped me find those questions. My journal let me complain, be happy, be upset, frustrated, whatever I was feeling about math or my life at the time, it would absorb, hold it for me, but allow me to free it from my system.

INTRODUCTION

This is me and math. It reads like a roller coaster ride. Parts of it reach heights of understanding, others fall into oblivion and at some points I am not sure what was going on. But if nothing else, there is potential in this journal. There is the potential of the student to understand the math, and there is the potential of this journal writing exercise to be a serious aid in that understanding.

CONCLUSION (CLOSING EVALUATION)

This journal has helped me to iron out difficulties as well as given me the chance to revel in my accomplishments. (Although that sentence is a grammatical failure, I think you probably catch my drift.) The journal writing method is a neat concept; perhaps I'll use it on my own at college.

Summary

Some purposes of journals:

- To increase confidence.
- To increase participation.
- To decentralize authority.
- To encourage independence.
- To replace quizzes and tests as a means of assessment.
- To monitor progress.

- To enhance communication between teacher and student.
- To record growth.

Some uses for journals:

- To focus attention to a topic at the beginning of a class.
- To start a discussion.
- To summarize.
- To respond to a speaker, film, reading.
- To practice cognitive skills—observing, speculating, questions, revising.

What to look for in and to expect from journals:

- Language that is informal, conversational, personal, and contextual.
- Questions, observations, doubts, digressions, examples, drawings, sketches.

What to measure when evaluating journals:

- Frequency of entries.
- Length.
- Self-initiated topics.

Some questions to stimulate journal entries:

- Define three terms from the textbook.
- What are you thinking?
- Explain what we are doing so a younger student will understand it.
- Write this again in a different way.
- What makes you certain?
- What does this formula mean? What does it say in English?
- Why does this step make sense?
- Are you stuck? What information do you need to get you unstuck?
- What makes the problem difficult?

Five

Word Problems and Problems with Words

Students (and some of their teachers) complain about having to do word problems in math class. Although I think I understand their distaste for the form, I have always felt that word problems had potential because they were closer to real mathematics than much of the rest of what is found in textbooks. Good problems provide occasions for informal and formal writing. For example, I have asked seventh graders to work on problems such as "How many squares are there on a checkerboard? How many rectangles?"

Usually we spend time in class exploring and discussing the problem, first as a class, then in small groups. Finally I ask students to write up the problem, responding to three questions:

- What is the problem? Describe it in your own words.
- What was your approach to the problem?
- What did you find out?

First drafts will be rough and incomplete, but final papers are expected to be neat and clear with a lot of illustrations and examples.

The Thirteen Factors Problem

Finding a number that has exactly thirteen factors is an excellent problem for middle school students who need to strengthen their number sense. Recognizing prime numbers, identifying factor pairs, appreciating the many ways that numbers like 17, 22, and 24 differ, is what Henry Pollack calls "learning the biography of the numbers."[1] I usually introduce the question with a letter to the editor that was published in *Mathematics Teaching* (March 1981, 7), the journal of the Association of Teachers of Mathematics of Great Britain.

Dear Sir,

I am writing to you about a mathematical problem. Last week in maths when we were doing some work on factors one of the questions that we were given was: "Can you find a number with 13 factors?" All our class tried to work it out. Even our teacher can't find one. We then talked about it. We have tried all the square numbers up to 20.

We know that if there is an answer it must be a square number, as only square numbers have an odd number of factors. We realize that there may not be a number with 13 factors, but who knows?

I hope that somebody can help us.

Wendy Savage
(age 14)
Northcliffe Comprehensive School, Doncaster

Perhaps the challenge of competition explains the interest in this problem among my students over the years. Certainly, Wendy Savage's suggestion that such a number may not exist does not deter them. Some questions that we consider in our initial discussion of this problem include:

- How many factors does 12 have? 24? 20? 6?
- What is a good definition of the term "prime number"?
- Which numbers have an odd number of factors? Explain.
- Suppose you were looking for a number with three factors. How would you find it?
- What about numbers with five or nine factors? Give examples and tell what they have in common.
- Which square has fifteen factors? Can you find another?

Tony, a seventh grader, described his exploration of the problem:

PRIME FACTORS—GETTING A NUMBER WITH 13 FACTORS

Our project, and problem, in my math class was to find a number with 13 factors. In going about this problem, the first thing that I discovered was that factors come in pairs, 2, 4. Since perfect squares have one pair of factors which includes the same number twice, then the number of factors a perfect square has is odd. After going about more research in the same area, I discovered that only perfect squares have an odd number of factors.

The next thing I did was make a list of the numbers to 20, and their squares. Then next to those numbers I wrote a list of the factors of the squares, and the number of factors that the number has. I noticed that all but one of the numbers with three factors was odd, but more interestingly that each of those numbers had a square root that was prime. A rule we concluded was that every number with a prime square root had three factors.

However, that still left the question of finding a number with 13 factors unanswered.

The next task I completed to reach the goal was to write out a list of the powers of two: 2, 4, 8, –. Next to those numbers we wrote the number of factors. I noticed that 2 had two factors, 4, three factors and so on. Through calculation (continuing the list farther) I discovered the number 4,096, the square of 64, had 13 factors.

Then there was a problem of getting a shortcut to find the number with 13 factors. I broke down the powers of 2 into their prime factors and discovered that a number with 2 prime factors had 3 factors, one with 3 primes had 4 factors, and so on. From there we deduced that 4,096 must have 12 prime factors since it had 13 factors.

Although Tony's detailed account is the work of a strong and articulate math student, he still struggles, in this essay, to put into words his insight about the powers of two. A more sophisticated mathematician, noticing that 2^2 (4) has three factors (1,2,4) and 2^3 (8) has four factors (1,2,4,8), would say that 2^n has $n + 1$ factors. Tony has clearly perceived this, but is not ready to state it in terse mathematical language. Nor would most seventh graders be ready to do so.

Here are two other students' written reports:

Our problem was to find a number with 13 factors. This is how our math class went about it:

To find this number our highly intelligible minds* knew a few things if we were to find this number. First, the number had to be a perfect square, the number would also have an odd number of factors. Second, the number's square had to be prime. Before we figured these clues out, we were randomly picking numbers from the top of our heads.

We looked at many numbers before we realized that if we doubled numbers (starting with the number one) it formed a steady pattern counting by ones. We kept doubling numbers and finding the number of factors until we reached the number that had 13 factors, which is. . . . .
     4096!!!   **Just joking!*
                                                      —Jenny

THIRTEEN FACTORS

Finding a number with thirteen factors was a perplexing problem that was solved by our class. We went through lists of numbers and recorded how many factors each number had. We then tried several square numbers and determined that a number with 13 factors had to be a perfect square. Because every odd number has 3 factors we knew that the number with 13 factors had to be an even perfect square. We arranged a table of the powers of 2 and their factors, and discovered that the number 4096 had thirteen factors, and was two to the thirteenth power.

In solving the problem, I learned many new things about the factorization of many different classes of numbers.

                                                      —Harry

Jenny and Harry both reveal misconceptions that might not have come out had they not produced written accounts of their work. Jenny says that the number's square had to be prime—an impossibility. She probably meant to say the number's square root had to be prime and that this was true of numbers with exactly three factors. Harry confuses this point as well, suggesting to me that more discussion was required.

Becky wrote a letter:

13:30 (army time)

Dear General Countryman:

The problem that faced us was a tough one! We had to figure out what square number had 13 factors. We approached it very carefully armed only with paper, pencils, and our brains! The first attempt we made was not to solve it but to gather info. For instance—one thing that we learned was that all numbers with 3 factors were 3 things: (a) All the numbers were odd (except 4) (b) the numbers were all squares and (c) the numbers' square roots are all prime. We did many charts and lists displaying what we figured out and discovered.

We finally made a list going up in "2's." We kept on going up until the R side reached 13 and then moved the L side up that many spaces. Thus resulting in the final answer:

L	R
4096	13

Yours sincerely
Corp. Becky

Ian wrote a more fanciful account of his work:

THE THIRTEENTH FACTOR

As I sat in my office on Saturday morning waiting for a case suddenly a sharp knock came upon my door.

"Come in," I called.

The door opened slowly and in came a man with a long overcoat and a hat. A shadow was cast over his face so it could not be seen. He slowly walked up to my desk and dropped an envelope on the desk.

"Read," he said.

I read, TOP SECRET GOVERNMENT INFORMATION: Find a number with 13 factors or the world is . . . Suddenly the paper burnt up. I imagined it was supposed to self destruct after a certain time period.

"Do you accept?" he asked.

"Yes."

"Good. Begin work immediately," he turned, began to walk out the door and said, "and swiftly."

I soon realized that the number had to be a perfect square, perfect squares being the only numbers with an odd number of factors since the square root would pair off with itself. The number's square root could not be a prime because all numbers squared from a prime would have three and only three factors.

Should I list every square number? No, too long and too much work. I've got it!! The perfect way. I figured that method out in my early days. Why didn't I think of it before? I will list all the numbers that are powers of two and the one to the twelfth power will have to have 13 factors!

Conclusion: the number 4096 was the one with 13 factors and I returned it to the government. What part it played in saving the world I don't know, but I'm still here today. I learned many things from this case, like how to find a number with any amount of factors and how to get a number with three factors (a prime²).

—Ian

The Emperor's Oats

I call one of my favorite problems "The Emperor's Banquet." I introduce it this way:

> You have been invited to the emperor's banquet. The emperor is a rather strange host. Instead of sitting with his guests at his large round dining table, he walks around the table pouring oats on the head of every other person. He continues this process, pouring oats on the head of everyone who has not had oats until there is only one person left. The question is, where should you sit if you do not want oats poured on your head?

"The Emperor's Banquet" requires considerable discussion and exploration. Students want to know how many guests will be at the banquet, whether the emperor sits down, whether he starts ar the same place and goes in the same direction, and whether the best solution is not to accept the invitation. My answers to these queries are that first of all, you never know how many other guests will appear, so you have to be prepared. The emperor never sits at his table, but he always starts at the same place and proceeds in the same direction, pouring oats on the head of every other person, and ignoring those people who have already had oats poured on their heads. Of course, an invitation to the emperor's house is a command performance and one would never refuse to attend. (Readers may want to explore the problem themselves before reading the discussion and solution that appear in the Appendix.)

During the course of their exploration of this problem I ask students to write up short accounts of their work. The examples that follow trace the progress of one group as they find patterns and make discoveries about a problem that initially seems much too difficult to solve.

Emperor Tangerini has invited me to a Masquerade Ball. But, instead of him eating, he comes around and pours oats on people's heads. He picks those people out who are in every other seat. He goes around as many times as possible until only one person is left. Ex: 12 people (1,3,5,7,9,11,2,6,10,4,12 ...... 8!!) I must sit in a place where I will be the last one. I do not know how many people are coming, so I must come up with a formula.

It is only one hour until the ball and me and my advisors have not figured out the solution. We have tried the 2 seat, the 4 seat, the 6 seat; formulas concerning doubles, triples, halves and thirds; and we still haven't come up with a solution. We need new advisors (I guess)?! Can you figure it out? We can't seem to.

—Noah

THE EMPEROR'S TABLE

This problem is explained like this: The emperor is having a banquet and for pleasure he dumps oats on people's heads. Once the oats have been dumped. The person who it was dumped on leaves the table. The person who is last at having oats dumped on his head wins. The question is where is the best place to sit.

It seems evident that this problem is different depending on whether the amount of people is odd or even. If the amount of people are even you should sit next to the first person that the oats are being dumped on. Make sure that if the king is going to the right side that you are sitting to the left of the first person that the oats will be dumped on. When the amount of people are odd you should try to sit directly opposite of the king. This is impossible but if you sit to the right side of the first person, and if the king is going left you should be okay.

—Sarah

EMPER'S TABLE

There is an emper who invites people over for dinner but when he has a party he doesn't eat. Instead he dumps porage on the head of every other person but he doesn't dump porage on the last person.

—Ben

Recently in Math Class I had to do a problem. This is it. You are invited to the Emperor's banquet. At the banquet the emperor pours oats over the guests. He does it like this—he pours oats over the person who is sitting in the first seat and then goes to the 3rd, then the 5th, and so on. If oats are spilled on you you get up and leave, but if not you remain.

The class is suppose to figure out which seat would be the last one to have oats poured on.

The way I approached this problem is I figured out which would be the last to be hit if their was 1 to 50 seats and wrote a chart to help me find a pattern.

Some of the things I figured out about this problem is: that the number is always even and I also found a pattern. The pattern is you start with 2 and square it then you write the even numbers up to it. Then you square 4 and do the same thing with the evens, then you square 8 and so on.

—David

THE EMPEROR'S BANQUET

Pretend you are invited to a banquet at the emperor's palace—but the problem is that it's rumored that instead of eating, the emperor himself pours oats on people's heads.

He pours them on every other person's head, and after you've gotten oats you have to leave. The last person doesn't get oats—so the question is—where should you sit?

At first I just fooled around with the numbers—then I went through and made a table of where you should sit with from 2 to 16 people.

# of people	# to sit at
The first thing I noticed	
2	2*
was that all the same	
3	2
numbers (*) were powers	
4	4*
of two.	
5	2
The next day I figured	
6	4
out the differences bet-	
7	6
ween the two numbers.	
8	8*

# of people	# to sit at
They were in order from	
9	2
2 to 16, 0,1,0,3,2,1,0,7,6,5,	
10	4
4,3,2,1,0	
11	6
After looking at these for	
12	8
a while I found a way to	
13	10
use the patterns to figure	
14	12
out where to sit.	
15	14
You should take the num-	
16	16*

ber of people, subtract the nearest power of 2 higher than the number of people then subtract the answer from the number of people.

Mercedes showed me another way. Take the number of people and subtract from it the closest power of 2 less than the number of people. Take that answer and multiply it by 2 and there's your seat to sit at.

—John

Words in Mathematics

When I first drafted this book, I was reluctant to use the phrase "word problem." The trouble with "word problem" is that it suggests that there is something different about mathematics when it is expressed in words. It is all words. The symbols that we associate with mathematics come not at the beginning but at the end of the long process of exploring, questioning, and challenging, of *doing* mathematics. Words are tools with which we think, and thinking is the central concern of mathematics teaching. Attending to words will help students learn mathematics better. Although we might disagree about the nature of mathematics, even that argument will take place in the context of language.

I used to ask my students to consider whether their answers made any sense; then I realized that for some students none of it made sense. When I looked at what I asked of students I came to see that for many of them my demands were arbitrary and confusing. There is the problem of mathematics words and ordinary words. Mathematics is a world of degrees, radicals, and imaginary numbers. Why are there right angles, but no left angles or wrong angles? No wonder students find mathematics mysterious.

Consider a typical algebra exercise: Find three consecutive odd integers such that the sum of the largest and twice the smallest is 25. Finding the solution is not difficult, but what language skills are necessary to produce it? What do *consecutive, odd*, and *integer* mean? What about *such that?* To what does the word *sum* refer?

Many of the words in mathematics are difficult for a student to decode, and learning to decode technical language is an important part of the process of learning mathematics. Daphne Kerslake, a British educator, points out the hazard of demanding the use of correct mathematical terminology. To a child who names a diamond, but does not see the rotation that will make the diamond a square, two different words are both natural and useful. Only confusion will result when the name is demanded before the idea is mastered. I have seen middle school students who recite that "all squares are rectangles but not all rectangles are squares" refuse to call a quadrilateral with equal sides and equal angles anything but a square. Definitions alone rarely throw much light on the ideas they represent. They are usually the end product of much exploration and careful thought. In fact, the precision of a definition belies the effort that has contributed to its formulation.

Students do not learn the same things in the same way. Even students with the same cultural and class backgrounds do not learn in the same way. In the best world, we construct our understanding of mathematics over many years, carefully fitting new experiences and insights into what we already know. Language minority students face additional difficulties, for it is easy to misinterpret the meaning of even fairly simple questions. In *Twice As Less*, Eleanor Wilson Orr points out the importance of prepositions and conjunctions—by, if, or, with, and for—little words that carry great meaning in mathematics.

> It may be that during a discussion of an algebraic fraction written on the blackboard, a student hears the teacher speak of dividing the quantity on the bottom of the fraction *into* the quantity on the top, and registers the order of the quantities: first the one on the bottom, then the one on the top. The student in turn uses this order, but not necessarily with an *into;* he or she may see no more reason to use an *into* with this order than a *by:* both of them are division prepositions. But from the perspective of standard English, if the student uses *by*, the direction of the division gets reversed. (1987, 84)

Orr urges teachers to attend to features of black English that can interfere with a student's learning mathematics and science.

How do students come to understand the mathematical meaning of words like *difference?* What is the *difference* between 7 and 4? What is the *difference* between a square and a rectangle? What is the *difference* between a horse and a pig? The word *fraction* means quotient in mathematics, fragment or part in ordinary English. What do they make of words like *irrational, imaginary,* and *mean* in mathematical English?

The National Assessment of Educational Progress reports that a large majority of students in grades seven and eleven feel that mathematics is rule-based, and about half of them say that learning mathematics is mostly memorizing. Language is both part of the problem and part of the solution. More talking, reading, listening, and writing, along with acting, doing, and constructing, will help students make sense of mathematics. If teachers shift away from simply presenting material and move toward promoting activity, they will make mathematics teaching more effective and more rewarding.

A language approach to the teaching of mathematics provides opportunities for students to develop listening, speaking, reading, and writing skills as they acquire mathematical knowledge. The typical lesson in algebra class focuses almost exclusively on the presentation of a problem type, followed by a sample demonstration, followed by student practice. A better approach would give students an opportunity to work together to solve problems, with the teacher explaining the various terms as they arise, listening for problematic language and math features, and asking discussion questions.

Summary

- Word problems can provide good opportunities for writing activities that promote mathematical inquiry.
- Writing about these problems encourages students to focus on their own thinking and use their own language.
- Students' difficulty with word problems is symptomatic of the larger problem of words and mathematics.
- Words are tools for thinking—in mathematics as in other disciplines.
- Conceptions and misconceptions will be revealed as students describe their explorations of a problem.
- Students will be able to explore multiple methods and multiple solutions.
- Students will become authors of their own ideas.
- Writing about their work gives students a chance to experience a creative side of mathematics.

Six

Formal Writing

Writing is a recursive not a linear process. The writer reflects on, returns to, and builds upon what has gone before. The stages of composition—prewriting, drafting, revising, editing, publishing—are interactive, and sometimes indistinct. Drafting and revising may occur simultaneously. Prewriting (the set of experiences that motivate writing) may well come as a result of revising.

A similar observation can be made about the stages of problem solving. Some researchers characterize those stages as:

1. Experiencing the phenomenon.
2. Stating the problem.
3. Constructing a mathematical model.
4. Manipulating algebraic statements.
5. Stating a solution.
6. Interpreting the solution in a mathematical context.
7. Interpreting the solution in the real world.

Stated this way problem solving looks like a linear process; but when mathematicians and other scientists are asked to describe their work, they present a much more complex process, one step leading backward as well as forward, questions generating new questions. What we know about composing and about problem solving suggests that students would do

Composition	Problem Solving
prewriting	experiencing the phenomenon
drafting	stating the problem
revising	constructing a mathematical model
editing	manipulating algebraic statements and stating a solution
publishing	interpreting the solution in a mathematical context; and interpreting the solution in the real world

Figure 6–1. Stages of composition and problem solving

well to build a repertoire of experiences that allows them to move comfortably among these activities in order to become good writers and good thinkers (see Figure 6–1).

The Writing Process

Many of the examples of student writing that appear in this book were produced during prewriting or experiencing-the-phenomenon classroom activities: talking, listening, observing, reading, freewriting, brainstorming, notetaking. Others come from the drafting or stating-the-problem stage, the time when the writer/problem solver, silencing the internal voice that wants to edit every phrase, produces connected prose. The purpose of these activities is to help students find out and record what they know.

Revising, the experience of re-viewing or re-making knowledge in response to new information, is a significant part of both processes. Editing is similar to manipulating and generating solutions. Publishing, which is akin to interpreting the solution in the mathematical and the real worlds, in the classroom means having students share their work. It can occur at any point in the process. Students can read journal entries to each other; listen to paper drafts; write letters to other classes, or younger students, or parents; write term papers; display their work; and produce newsletters or books.

Publication can take many different forms, as the following examples illustrate. Matt Barker, a junior at Eisenhower High School in Yakima, Washington, wrote a letter to the Coca-Cola company after a problem-solving session in his precalculus class:

Yakima, Washington

The Coca-Cola Co.
310 North Ave. NW
Atlanta, GA 30313

Dear Roberto:

How can it be that both Coke and "the other one" are both the soft drink chosen in a taste test? I personally am a devoted Coke drinker. Coke Classic is #1!

There is something that has been bothering me. Our precalculus class at Eisenhower High School was given the problem of finding the can that would hold 12 fl. oz. and would use the least amount of aluminum. Much to our surprise, the can we discovered is much different from the one you chose! Our calculations show that a can with a radius of approximately 3.8367 cm and a height of approximately 7.667 cm would use less aluminum than yours and still hold 12 fl. oz. Please explain why you still choose to use more aluminum than is necessary. I doubt that you want to lose money, and I hate to see valuable resources go to waste (I recycle). I feel it would be to your benefit to change the size of the can, help conserve resources, and save money all in one fell swoop!

Something else is on my mind: Cherry Coke was a smashing success! But what about those of us who love vanilla Coke? Now that Burger Ranch has stopped adding vanilla syrup to their Coke, where are we to go?

How about if you created vanilla Coke for all of us? You don't even have to tell anybody that I gave you the idea. It will be my little gift to you!

You will make billions. Pepsi—oops, I said the "P" word—will not be notified.

Cordially,
Matt Barker, Junior
Eisenhower High School

(Quoted in Crosswhite et al., 1989, 669)

The perfunctory reply from Coca-Cola, a form letter, did not deter Matt's enthusiasm.

Derrick, an eleventh grader enrolled in an algebra class designed for students whose background in math was not strong enough for the precalculus course, produced a lengthy journal entry one day in response to my suggestion that he write something about the law of sines (see Figure 6–2). Derrick's statement is remarkable in many ways. First, he sets out to *prove* the law of sines, a task that would never occur to me as an assignment for this group of students. Second, he asserts that he wants to show that the law is reasonable. How many math students learn to prove statements without ever considering whether or not they are reasonable? Indeed, how many prove statements that they themselves feel make no sense whatsoever? Finally, Derrick succeeds in writing a statement that, while it will need editing, is nonetheless well on the way to being a respectable proof of the law of sines.

Papers

A paper? How could you have a paper in math?? I guess it seems to some people that math is a subject of figures and calculations and answers, simple concise answers, certainly leaving no room for discussion. This year has really helped shatter my concept of mathematics. . . . It has been very challenging.

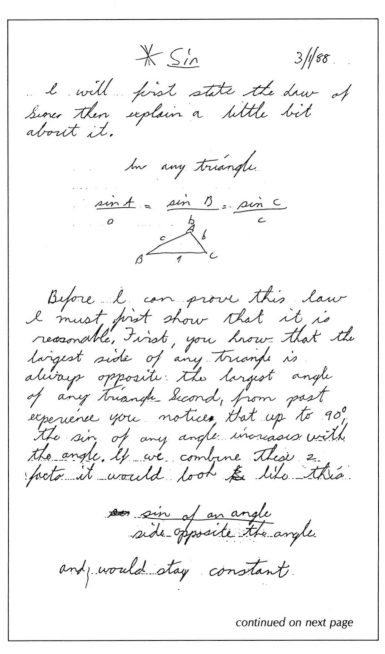

$$\frac{\sin A}{a} = \frac{\sin B}{b} = \frac{\sin C}{c}$$

Figure 6–2. Derrick on the law of sines

continued from previous page

I will now prove the law of sines. This law can be applied to acute as well as obtuse triangles.

A perpendicular with an altitude from A cutting BC
  – Altitude is h.
  – Base meeting altitude will be called D.

$$\sin A = \frac{h}{b} \quad or \quad b \cdot \sin A = h$$
$$\sin B = \frac{h}{a} \quad or \quad a \cdot \sin A = h$$

Therefore $b \sin A = h = a \sin B$

or

$$\textcircled{b} \sin A = \textcircled{a} \sin B$$

Then divide by ab.

$$\frac{\sin A}{a} = \frac{\sin B}{b}$$

Similarly we can get

$$\frac{\sin A}{c} = \frac{\sin C}{c}$$

or

$$\frac{\sin B}{b} = \frac{\sin C}{c}$$

Therefore $\dfrac{\sin A}{a} = \dfrac{\sin B}{b} = \dfrac{\sin C}{C}$

In conclusion, the law of sines is a very convenient? conventional method of solving obtuse as well as acute angles. This is very good. Demich

Years ago I offered a course for students who might never explore any ideas in mathematics because they were never good enough in math to enroll in an advanced section. The audience for the class included the bored, the weak, and the frustrated students who always saw themselves in the "dumb section." Many signed up for Math 11V in a last (and many of them thought futile) attempt to find something good in the subject. Most in the class had completed two years of algebra and one of geometry. The course was elective, since the school required math only through Algebra II, but many students felt, and stated, an obligation to "take math to prepare for the SATs."

When I designed the course I had in mind my nonmathematician adult friends, many of whom never went near anything mathematical after high school. Consequently, they missed exploring any of the compelling material that I had encountered in college and graduate school. I might have called the course "Interesting Things I Happen to Know About Mathematics," but I was concerned with more than content. I knew that the climate of the classroom was as important as the syllabus, and that my teaching methods had to be consistent with group dynamics and personal histories.

The study of mathematics sets complex emotional traps for students and teachers. Almost everyone is frightened at some point by the logical structure of the discipline: the rigor, and the always compelling search for right answers. When I started teaching math I decided to confront that fear by creating a supportive climate in the classroom. I told students that I expected them to help each other—in class, on homework, on tests, in every activity. I said that the final test of whether they had learned any math was their ability to teach it to someone else. Group process and communication have always been central concerns in my classes, as important as the details of the quadratic formula. Although the approach succeeded in building the confidence of some students, many remained fearful, and few were inspired by textbooks filled with practice exercises.

The amount of ground covered in Math 11V depended a great deal on student energy and interest. Some years we delved into every chapter of the text, a popular work called

Mathematics and the Imagination (Kasner and Newman, 1989), reviewed algebra and geometry, and indulged in a crash course in basic trigonometry. Other years we barely managed discussing Zeno's paradox, exploring topology, and reviewing for the achievement tests.

Independent projects were a major component every year, however. I expected every student to explore and report on two or three topics in mathematics. I tried to define mathematics broadly enough to encompass student interests. The scientists among them struggled with relativity; the musicians read about Pythagorean harmony; the artists explored the work of M. C. Escher.

Initially, many students thought a math project was ridiculous. Since they felt that they "couldn't possibly do math" on their own, they could not imagine exploring, researching, and reporting on anything mathematical. In the end, most said that the projects were the most satisfying part of the course. They did produce remarkable work, especially those who tried to write about mathematics for younger students, usually involving something they had learned during the year. I made lists of topics (see Figure 6–3) to help students get started, and I had them give oral presentations as well as written reports of their findings. "Don't bore us," I advised students on their presentations. "We need not hear everything you learned, just a fascinating instance." My admonition inspired lively moments of talk and examples of artistic display.

The formal papers were another matter, however. I dreaded sitting down to read and grade the stacks of barely disguised, reconstructed encyclopedia essays. My warning about not boring the class did not inspire them to consider the plight of the teacher as reader. Indeed, since I was the only reader, students seemed content with the standard approach to term papers: try to impress the teacher with maximum volume and minimum effort. I loved hearing their class presentations, and I hated reading their work. The best solution, it seemed to me at the time, was to abandon the term paper. I thought that formal writing just would not work, even in an unconventional math class.

Many years later, pleased with the results of informal writing activity, and inspired by Ken Macrorie's ideas about student research as he described them in *Searching Writing*

African Mathematics	Paradoxes and Logic
Ancient Math	Pascal's Theorem
Computation Systems	Perfect Numbers
Computer Programming	Prime Numbers
Conic Sections	Projective Geometry
Divisibility	Puzzles and Card Tricks
Fermat's Last Theorem	Pythagoreans
Fibonacci Numbers	Regular Polygons
Finite Differences	Polyhedrons
Flatland and the Fourth Dimension	Relativity
Flexagons	Soap-Bubble Geometry
Four-Color Problem	Tesseleations
Golden Section	Topology
Koenigsberg Bridge Problem	Transcendental Numbers
Nomographs	Triangle Trigonometry
Paper Folding	Vectors

Figure 6–3. Possible topics for a math paper

(1988), I decided to ask students in an advanced math class to write a "math search" paper. I worked with them on choosing a topic, gave them class time to write drafts, and put them in small groups for editing and rewriting. The result was a collection of lively and readable papers.

We started by brainstorming lists of possible topics. There were questions that had arisen in the course of our work in calculus—the notion of limit, transcendental numbers, exponential functions. There were topics that they had explored in other years—conic sections, prime numbers, Pascal's triangle. There was interest in looking at mathematics as part of the general culture—the calendar, gambling, numerology, nutrition. I suggested that they spend a few days thinking about what they wanted to know, writing notes, discussing topics with parents and friends. I wanted them to look for their own deep interests.

Sarah, for example, chose to explore a question about population growth in China:

This paper was stimulated by the idea that a good way to control population would be to allow couples to have as many children as they wished until they had a boy, at which point they would be required to stop. When I first thought about this suggestion I was intrigued with the social, moral, and philosophical problems it posed rather than the mathematical ones.

Once they selected a topic I had them discuss it with other members of the class. They were to ask for help: tips, names of people who might be helpful, books, magazines, etc. I asked them to keep notes on all of this exploration. I suggested that they think about interviewing people who knew about the topic, and that they generate lists of appropriate questions. Sarah's initial questions helped frame her paper.

Would there eventually be more females than males in the society?
Would this be an effective form of population control?
Would it be overly effective?
What would the economic effects of a baby crash (as opposed to a baby boom) be?

The research process took place during two months in the spring term. In early April we began to discuss subjects. By the middle of the month the students had selected their topics, and on the day these were declared we spent fifteen minutes freewriting in class. I asked the students to write the title and the first page of the paper. Of course there were strong and loud objections to this task, but the exercise provided a powerful way for students to find their own questions.

Source Day followed, a class session devoted to looking at and exchanging resources. Students read one another's draft questions and comments and looked through books and articles provided by other students and by me. A first draft was due one week later, and on that day I had them read and comment on one another's work. A second draft was due in early May; again students reviewed and edited the work of their classmates.

To assist with the construction of the paper I gave them questions:

1. What did you know, and what did you not know, when you started this paper?
2. Why are you writing this paper?
3. Tell the story of the search. What did you do to find out and how?
4. What did you learn, and what did you not learn?

Responding to #2, Sarah wrote:

I chose this as my paper topic for a few different reasons: (a) I couldn't think of a topic more interesting, (b) population is a real, genuine problem. It is out there in the world waiting to be solved. One of my biggest problems with math as a subject is a distaste for solving equations for their own sake and not understanding what purpose a solution might serve.

The story of her search included this explanation of a hypothetical case:

Assume that every woman has children at the rate of one a year, starting at age eighteen and continuing until she either has a boy or has her eleventh child at age twenty-eight: If we take a sample of 128 couples for example:

128	can have 1st child,	64 will have boys,	64 will have girls
64	2nd	32	32
32	3rd	16	16
16	4th	8	8
8	5th	4	4
4	6th	2	2
2	7th	1	1
1	8th	*- 50 % chance -*	

127 boys   127 girls
1 that could be either

We devoted a total of four class days and one extended freewriting session to this effort. In late May I received a stack of lively and readable term papers. Sarah's paper concluded:

> *It is important to recognize a few of the many limitations of this kind of study. My analysis treats population shrinkage as an isolated process, one without a social setting of any kind. The number I came up with could be affected by natural resources, economic growth, social mobility, and family norms. . . . Population policies similar to the no children after a boy rule have been implemented in both India and China. In China, families are strongly encouraged to have only one child and in India thousands of people have been sterilized. Both countries knew that the fertility rate would naturally go down if living standards went up, but decided that they could not afford to wait for educational and economic gains to take effect; neither country had the resources to feed its ever growing populations, let alone educate and employ them.*

I read narratives about prime numbers and probability, the fourth dimension, and *pi*. I learned that "a sunflower does not try to grow its seeds so that they fit the Fibonacci series, rather the easiest place for the seeds to grow leads them to form the series." In "Alice in Integrationland" I found some of the implications of the intermediate value theorem:

> *Alice decided that she was going to have to find someone who could tell her how to get home. She was tired of being scolded for not understanding calculus (as it really was a difficult subject).*
> *Soon she came to a sign which read:*

> Welcome to the House
> of
> Intermedius

> *As Alice desperately wanted someone to talk to, she decided to see whether anyone was home. Timidly she knocked on the door. To her surprise it creaked open. Alice looked around the room, which was empty except for a flight of stairs.*

"Is anyone at home?" she asked.

A small voice replied, "I'm on the third floor." So Alice climbed the flight of stairs and then another until she reached the third floor. When she arrived there was a smaller creature waiting for her.

"Hello, my name is Alice."

"Mine is Intermedius."

"What a strange sounding name," said Alice rather rudely.

Very coldly, the creature replied, "It is the diminutive of my proper name, Intermediate Value Theorem. But my friends call me Intermedius. You do know that that means don't you?" he asked. Alice who did not know, did not reply.

"Well, it means that if you have two numbers and if you want to get from one to the other it is necessary to pass through all the ones in between. You came in my house on the first floor and I told you to come to the third—it was necessary for you to pass through the second."

"Perhaps," said Alice rather boldly, "you could tell me how I can get home."

I was so pleased with the results that I decided to include a formal paper as a requirement in all of my advanced mathematics classes. The assignment is to write a paper describing the student's exploration of a topic of interest. The investigation should involve some aspect of the year's work but the first concern is that the topic should be something the student cares about. For example, Hanna was interested in teaching and learning:

There are many stereotypes about mathematics: children do not like it, boys are better at it and so on. Many of these stereotypes do not hold true in the classroom. The goal of this project was to see if there is a correlation between age or sex or the child's attitude toward math and how well first grade students were able to transfer mathematical knowledge of three digit addition and subtraction of money.

A group of twenty-two first grade students were given a questionnaire which provided the data of this project. The questionnaire asked if the children liked math, if they found math hard or easy. The students had completed surveys like

*this one in the past and were accustomed to the format.
They were also uninhibited to tell their true feelings. The
survey then had ten problems of addition and subtraction
of money (dollars and cents.) The children have been doing
three digit addition and subtraction for months using only
numbers without the dollar signs and the decimal point.
Their teacher expressed her confidence that all of the children could score 90% or higher on a simple test of addition
or subtraction problems. When the signs were added, however, only twelve children were able to score a 90% or
higher.*

Hanna found that while all the children reported that
they liked math, girls scored lower than the boys on the test.
She posed this question: If the children have the same attitude about math, then why do they score differently on tests?
Another student, Jon, was interested in collecting his
own data and studying some properties that he had learned
in physics. He decided to examine the behavior of bouncing balls.

*[I wanted] specifically to establish a relationship between
the height from which a ball is dropped and the height that
it then bounces. While I worked on this project, I also
became interested in the time over which a ball continues
to bounce, and I added my investigations in this area to
my paper.*

Jon found an exponential function to describe the relationship between the height from which the ball was dropped
and the time it stopped bouncing. He then commented that
few equations in Newtonian physics involve logarithms, for
most relations are either direct, inverse, or quadratic. In his
conclusion he posed questions about balls with different
masses, volumes, and materials and suggested avenues of further inquiry.
Aliza's comments on the experience of writing a paper in
a math course reflect student sentiment in general:

*I guess you've heard it lots of times now, but I really liked
the idea of the paper. Well, actually I didn't at first, but as*

I wrote it I really understood so much more. I guess that's what writing is for. . . . I guess the trick is that once you understand the point of something, stuff you may have done before takes on a new light; instead of knowing how *and* what *and just performing tasks, one can know* why *as well and really get stuff done. Would you say I've figured out your secret?*

Summary

- Composition and problem solving are similar processes. Both involve what mathematicians call recursive activity.
- Writing process activities—prewriting, drafting, revising, editing, publishing—help students develop thinking skills.
- Publication can take many forms—letters, papers, posters, displays, skits.
- Formal term papers can be a significant part of a mathematics course, but it is important for the teacher to pay attention to the process of developing the papers.

Seven

Evaluation and Testing

When I talk with teachers about writing in math they always ask about evaluation.

- We already have so much to cover. Are we just adding to the work load by assigning essays and papers that will take even longer to grade than the usual math homework?
- When will we have time to read all those journals?
- Math teachers don't know how to grade essays anyway. Will we have to become English teachers?

Reading and evaluating all the material produced in writing-oriented mathematics classes does sound onerous. The challenge for teachers is to find ways of acknowledging, affirming, and promoting student work without becoming mired in a sea of ungraded papers. Nonetheless, most teachers say that reading a set of student journals takes less time than they expected, and that they find the prose compelling. Journal entries help teachers understand their students' conceptions and misconceptions about the material. Papers show students' interest and concerns. Writing can also be a useful assessment tool, informing teachers about their students' understanding and fluency.

I think of the assessment process as an ongoing conversation between teacher and students about mathematical ideas. Periodic assessment helps me make decisions about pacing, direction, content, and methods. Although the most common form of evaluation is testing to assign grades, assessment is more than just the administration of quizzes and tests; it is continuous and dynamic, and its purpose is to promote learning. Writing in mathematics can be a significant part of this effort.

Writing can help teachers answer specific questions about students.

- Do students use math to make sense of complex situations?
- Can they formulate hypotheses?
- Can they organize information?
- Are they able to explain concepts?
- Can they use computation skills in context?
- Do they use mathematical language appropriately?
- Are they confident about using mathematical procedures?

Reading a few journal entries can help a teacher discover what the class understands.

Comments on the graphs of $y = b^x$ *and* $y = (1/b)^x$. *These two graphs are the same but reflected over the y-axis. Algebra shows us that this is true:*

$$(1/b)^x = (b^{-1})^x = b^{-x}$$

b^x *and* b^{-x} *are symetric about the y-axis, as are* b^x *and* $(1/b)^x$. *This happens only when* $b > 0$.

Why is b *positive? The reason is that when squaring a negative number it is positive and when it is cubed it is negative. Raised to the 4th it is positive, 5th negative, etc. et cetera. Therefore we are beset with a whole lot of parts that do not connect because* b^x *never can cross the x-axis.*

Rebecca has a clear sense that exchanging positive and negative values for x in the exponential function $y = b^x$ will produce a reflection through the y-axis. Her discussion about the need for the base, b, to be positive is less confident. It sounds like inner speech, her mind reviewing the behavior of negative numbers.

> *I find the fact that log_b x = y is the inverse of y = b^x very interesting. Were logarithms invented as a process by which you can solve for y in the equation x = b^y? In normal algebraic processes this is impossible. What exactly does a log do and why and how did it come about? . . . One more question, what in the world is base 1, what is base?*

My reply to this journal entry began with the last question.

> *"Base" refers to the base of the logarithm. For example log_{10} 10 = 1 hence (10,1); log_2 2 = 1 hence (2,1) and so on.*
> *Log$_b$ y = x implies that b^x = y. A logarithm is an exponent (notice the equation says log equals x, and x is the exponent in the second equation . . .)*

The question about the invention of logarithms reminded me that we needed more discussion in class about the history of logs and log functions.

Some writing—autobiographies and journal entries, for example—should not be graded or evaluated, although students should receive credit for their work. They appreciate comments and replies to their questions and comments, and I find it helpful to record in my gradebook the frequency and length of entries, and to make note of significant questions or topics. I do not evaluate writing style or look for mechanical errors in journals.

Essays, term papers, word problems, and investigations require evaluation, but a simple grading plan is often just as effective as a more elaborate scheme. After explaining my grading system to the class, I usually separate papers into three groups. In one I put papers where students "got the point"; the second pile is for those that "wrote something special"; in the third group are those that "missed the boat." It does not take long to characterize papers in this way, and students still learn what they want to know: How did I do? I return informal papers with the symbol check ($\checkmark$), plus ($+$), or minus ($-$) at the top of the first page.

In California, a new mathematics assessment includes open-ended questions for students in grade 12. These are questions in which students are asked to respond in writing to a mathematical situation. To evaluate the responses the assessment program uses a "general scoring rubric"[1] that sorts papers first into three categories: competent, satisfactory, or inadequate. Each of these groups is then further subdivided so that each paper receives one of six possible grades. Readers use a table (see Figure 7-1) to assist in the evaluation of student work.

In "The Argument for Writing Across the Curriculum" Toby Fulwiler (1986) offers some guidelines for teachers on commenting on student writing. I find this advice, which comes from the comments of many teachers who use writing in their practice, very helpful. Let me just sum up those guidelines in very condensed form:

- Respond to content rather than mechanics. Much of the writing that students do for you is (or should be) an act of communication.
- A positive and personal response will encourage students to revise and edit when necessary.
- Grades are not always necessary. They are certainly not appropriate on journal entries or early drafts, only on a finished paper.
- Single out one or two points to comment on rather than overwhelming the student with a large number of negative points.
- Be specific when you comment on a problem.
- Edit only a page or two. Let the student do the work of editing the entire paper. If you red pencil it the student won't have any work to do. If you indicate what bothers you and ask the student to use your advice as an example for editing the rest of the work, he or she will get more out of the editing process.
- Use peer editing and evaluation. Editing is a good way to improve writing skills, and students will learn from reading and evaluating one another's papers.

COMPETENT

Exemplary response—6 points
Clear, coherent, elegant; communicates effectively to the iden-tified audience; identifies all the important elements

Competent response—5 points
Reasonably clear; communicates effectively; identifies the most important elements

SATISFACTORY

Minor flaws—4 points
Completes the problem, the explanation is muddled; incom-plete argument; understands underlying mathematical ideas

Serious flaws—3 points
Begins problem but fails to complete or omits significant parts; inappropriate strategy; major computational errors

INADEQUATE

Begins but fails to complete—2 points
Explanation is not understandable; no understanding of the problem situation

Unable to begin effectively—1 point
Misrepresents the problem situation; copies parts of problem without attempting solution

No attempt—0 points

Figure 7–1. The general scoring rubric in use in California

- In class, discuss examples of good and bad writing with your students.
- Read out loud from student papers you consider good. Explain why you like them.

Many groups are exploring new forms of assessment in mathematics. The major concerns that shape the discus-sion are recognition of the narrowing influence of standard-ized testing and questions about the impact of technology. While standardized tests provide a relatively inexpensive way to evaluate large groups of students, most of these tests emphasize lower-order skills—computation rather than problem solving, for example. It is important to keep in mind that what is tested is what will be taught, however, and many mathematics educators believe that real change in the mathematics classroom will come only when the tests are revised.

All of the mathematics reform statements remind us that the tests have enormous impact on what we teach. For example, *Everybody Counts* (1989), the report of the Mathematical Sciences Advisory Board, argues:

> We must ensure that tests measure what is of value, not just what is easy to test. If we want students to investigate, explore, and discover, assessment must not measure just mimicry mathematics. By confusing means and ends, by making testing more important than learning, present practice holds today's students hostage to yesterday's mistakes. (70)

Technology is also beginning to have an impact on the curriculum and on testing. The introduction of calculators, graphing calculators, and computers at all grade levels, and recent decisions to allow calculator use on tests like the SAT and the College Board Mathematics Achievement tests foreshadow more radical change in what happens in math classrooms. The changes that are proposed emphasize thinking and conceptual skills over rote learning.

How might new forms of assessment promote learning in mathematics classes? In *Assessment Alternatives in Mathematics* (Stenmark, 1989), the California Mathematics Council suggests that we need to evaluate

- the use of mathematics to make sense of complex situations
- work on extended investigations
- the ability to formulate and refine hypotheses, collect and organize information, explain concepts orally and in writing, work with poorly defined problems or problems with more than one answer similar to those in real life

- the extent of understanding or misunderstanding about mathematical concepts
- the ability to define and formulate problems
- whether students question possible solutions, looking at all possibilities. (4–5)

Multiple-choice tests provide little information in these areas. We need to find instruments that will provide better evidence.

Recently, I started an eleventh-grade precalculus class by handing the students a paper that said:

> Write a five question test on composition of functions. You may use any materials, notes, etc., and you may consult with one other person in the class.

The students had come to class expecting to *take* a test. Their reaction at first was mixed. A few of them said, "You are so nice!" Others were wary. "Do we have to answer the questions?" I replied that the questions should have answers. "Yes, but do we have to give the answers?" they wanted to know.

My response was an enigmatic smile. I hoped to engage them in the real work of inquiry, the search for good questions. There was a quiet murmur in the room. Two girls had a discussion about inverse functions. One student helped another sort out the definitions of the terms *domain* and *range*. Another student insisted that his graphing question was more interesting than the one his partner had written.

Forty minutes later I received a dozen tests.

- *Graph f° g when* $f(x) = |x|$ *and* $g(x) = x^2 - 4$.
- *Write a brief essay on how the graph of f° g is different from the graph of* $x^2 - 4$. *How do the domain and range differ?*
- *Using decomposition, graph* $y = \sqrt{1/|x| + {}^{-}1}$. *Describe each step.*

As I read this set of very good questions I realized that I wanted to know more about how the students felt about writing a test. The next day I asked them to write about the experience.

At first I felt relief. Then I got nervous again when I thought I wouldn't know what to make up. I chose to work with someone in my group who always understands everything because I figured if I couldn't think of anything he would be able to. This process of making up a test showed me that I understood a lot more than I thought I did. I felt that I knew as much as my partner and that we had equal input. When I left the room after handing in my test I felt confident that I did understand the material and that I would continue to understand new material. I think making up our own test was a great idea.

Many students mentioned relief, reduced anxiety, and greater confidence in their abilities as a result of the test-writing exercise. Some expressed concerns about grades, and many found the new approach disquieting.

My opinion on the new type of test depends on how it is graded. I'm not saying that the grade is everything, but I am saying that I'm confused as to what this really was.

I thought that writing a test instead of taking one was a good assignment, but a hard one to grade.

I don't see how that can be considered a test or how it could be graded.

But some found themselves gaining new insights about the material:

It was interesting to look at the graphs of the functions we used. For instance, the graph of $\sqrt{\sin x}$ was nothing like what we had expected and we still cannot completely explain why it looks the way it does.

[Making up the test] forced me to pull together the chapter and find every kind of example of composition. I also got to see what parts of the chapter were most important, for I had to decide what exactly to ask for in each problem.

Others learned something about composing a test:

What really struck me about writing a test was how hard it was to include all aspects of composition on it. . . . You need a good sense of the subject matter to create a test.

While writing the test I found myself mentally reviewing problems that I had done before that I found interesting or informative. After this mental review I was more comfortable with my understanding of the subject and its patterns, methods, etc. I produced a test that I knew was challenging, but also one which I would have enjoyed taking.

And some students wrote about teaching and learning:

I guess I got a taste of what being a teacher is. . . . I was confused as to what was required—hard questions, duplicated questions, question to lead to question? I confused my partner a great deal. I confused myself. There really is a great difference between answering a set of questions and having the whole subject laid down in order to find questions—like a needle in a haystack.

As I read the comments I realized that by asking my students to write a test, to find the questions in the haystack, I was sharing a significant part of my experience with them. Teachers learn by explaining, and by searching for questions. Writing to learn gives students that opportunity.

It was really afterward that the exercise stayed with me. I thought of at least 2 ways to make a problem better. A regular test would not have remained in my mind. . . .

I found myself asking how a test can teach, and what kind of problems teach something. Do they have to be extra difficult, or is the point to make a test that is composed of problems that we can all do? What combination of the two is best?

My gradebook used to look like a standard list of names, numbers, and letter grades. At the end of each marking period I struggled to weigh and summarize each student's performance on homework and an array of quizzes and tests in order to produce a single grade and a comment. A noteworthy example, a technique skillfully executed, or a thoughtful contribution in class might pop into my head as I typed the report card. With luck, I might have made a note about the student in the margin of the gradebook. Chances were that I had forgotten to record anything, and the letters and numbers seldom jogged my memory.

Over the years I began to add checks, pluses, and minuses to the letters and numbers in the gradebook, then short notes about writing. Now, in addition to my record keeping, my students keep all of their work in a portfolio and hand it in to me at the end of a marking period. I ask them to put the papers in some sort of order, and to write a brief account of what they have included, and why. Sometimes I ask them to list all the topics they have learned, what pleases them, and what they still need to work on. In addition to being enormously helpful to my report card writing, this method of self-assessment builds confidence as it informs students about their progress.

Somehow I understand stuff that we'd done before better this year. Like last year (or wherever I learned it) I could do it, but I didn't get it, and now I understand what's going on.

Summary

- Evaluation of student writing need not take an enormous amount of time.
- Writing can be a useful assessment tool, one that informs the teacher about individual progress and about the progress of the class as a whole.
- Not all student work needs to be graded, but students should be given credit for what they do.
- A simple sorting rubric—for example dividing papers into three categories: competent, satisfactory, inadequate—is usually sufficient for evaluating papers.

- Comments should respond to content, not mechanics, of writing.
- Students can be good editors for one another.
- New forms of assessment, influenced by developments in testing and new technology, can broaden the classroom experience for students and teachers.

Eight

Reflections in the Classroom

Reading what students write when they write about math has given me a vision of the mathematics classroom as "a place where there is an open invitation to be thoughtful" (Silver et al., 1991, ix). Indeed, writing seems to promote the thoughtfulness that echoes in these voices.

> *Finding the domains and ranges of functions is really hard. Is there a mathematical way to do it or do you just do trial and error? I can usually get them but I am never confident because using trial and error you are bound to forget when "trying" numbers. For example, what would the domain of* $f(x) = \sqrt{|x|} + x/x+1$ *be? How is anyone supposed to figure something like that out?*
>
> *Is the range always related to the domain? Yes, that's a dumb question. Range is much easier to find out because all you have to do is figure out* $y = f(x)$.

As they record their questions, reflect, and muse about the work, my students give me insights on how they make sense of mathematics.

> *I have a question about horizontal asymptotes. I do not understand how a horizontal asymptote can still be an asymptote when a line passes through it. Could you please explain how this is? (I was going to draw a diagram show-*

ing what I don't understand, but when I tried to draw it, I got confused as to what type of function has a horizontal asymptote.) Does the function $y = 1/x - 2$ *have a horizontal asymptote at* $y = 0$? *If I take the inverse of that function I get* $x = 1/y + 2$. *If* $y = 0$ *then that function becomes undefined. What about the function* $y = 1/x - 2$? *If I take the inverse of that I get* $x = 1/(y + 2)$. *Would the horizontal asymptote be at* $y = {}^-2$? *If* $y = {}^-2$, *then the function is undefined. I graphed this on my calculator (I finally figured out how to use p-max and p-min) and I found that the function does indeed go through the asymptote. Why is this?*

Writing to learn is different from writing to show that you have learned what the teacher or the text has set for you to learn. As you write, ideas come to you. When students freewrite in math they can explore questions that lurk in the recesses of their minds. At the least, writing can be a way to find out what they know and what they do not know about a subject. I have noticed that informal writing encourages students to struggle with new material, to let themselves wonder, speculate, and experiment with ideas. Writing down these speculations makes a record of them, and allows students to look back on something of their own making. In this entry Sarah, an eleventh grader, explores the number *e*.

What about e?
$(1 + 1/n)^n$ *On my calculator, when I input* 10^{11} *as* n *I get* 2.718 *... but when I input* 10^{12} *I get one! Is that the point? When* $1/n$ *is too small for the calculator to imagine the formula becomes* $(1)^n = 1$?
That's strange, one (1) must be so frustrated, it can never get any bigger, but the teensiest bit bigger than one (aided of course by the fact that the exponent is that much bigger) can [change] the number from 1 to 2.718 ...

It sounds like poetry. There is poetry, too, in a seventh grader's observations about area and perimeter.

1. *Find some examples of rectangles with the perimeter of 20. Then find out what happens to the area of the rectangles. Which area is biggest? Which is smallest?*

2. *What I did was I drew up 9 rectangles all with different combinations of width and length which had a perimeter of 20.*

3. *Even though all the perimeters were the same all of the areas are different. The rectangle with the largest area was number 2. The one with the smallest area was #1. I noticed that when the width and the length were closer together in dimensions the area was bigger. When the numbers were one small and one large the area tended to be lower. Another way to show this information is a chart. See below.*

Width	Length	Perimeter	Area
1	*9*	*20*	*9*
1 1/4	*8 3/4*	*20*	*10.93*
1 1/2	*8 1/2*	*20*	*12.75*
2	*8*	*20*	*16*
2 1/2	*7 1/2*	*20*	*18.75*
3	*7*	*20*	*21*
3 1/2	*6 1/2*	*20*	*22.75*
3 3/4	*6 1/4*	*20*	*23.43*
4	*6*	*20*	*24*
5	*5*	*20*	*25*

An eleventh grader discovers that what he knows about quadratics does not tell him what he wants to know about a cubic function.

I wish $x = {}^{-}b/2a$ worked on the box problem. Maybe there is some different formula for that but I forget how we got this one. I guess I could look at the equation and look at the maximums. Maybe there isn't one. It means very little unless one plans on spending large parts of one's life studying boxes. Does that make one a boxologist? It doesn't matter I guess since it is such a rare occurrence, the little hump on some $y = x^3$ junk type graph.

Twenty years ago, as a classroom teacher struggling to convey to my students the central points of high school mathematics, I had no chart to guide me in the murky realm of thinking and learning. I was lucky to discover writing, for the words of my students helped me think about the climate of the classroom, about mathematics in the real world, and about how to nurture the habit of learning.

The Classroom Climate

Writing in the classroom means that everyone is active. With talk, whether it be lecture or discussion, only one person is speaking at a time. The rest of the people in the room may participate by active listening and notetaking, but it is easy for some students to disengage, or let the few who dominate the class do all the work. Writing first and then talking about what was written means that everyone participates and more collaboration among students is possible. At the end of these collaborations students can write descriptions of what has transpired. Here Ellen explains what her group found out about triangular numbers:

> *I'm writing to explain the discovery I and a couple of my colleagues have found. The discovery is that now we know how to find triangular numbers. First of all a triangular number is a number that can be put into the shape of a triangle. The way you find a triangular number is you multiply n × (n + 1) ÷ 2 = the first n's triangular number. For example if I wanted to find the triangular number of 12, I would multiply 12 × 13 = 156 ÷ 2. So 78 is the triangular number of 12.*
> *I hope you find this useful.*

John summarizes his work on finding the areas of closed figures constructed on a geoboard:

> *About a week ago we started looking at geoboard figures and finding the area of them. We started with simple squares, rectangles and triangles. We found that with right triangles you could just multiply the length by the width and divide it by 2. We then started to try to find a rule that would find the area of all geoboard shapes.*

I discovered that all shapes with 12 dots on the outside and 3 inside have an area of 8. All shapes with 12 outside and 4 inside have an area of 9. All with 5 inside have an area of 10. It follows then that with all shapes that have 12 dots on the outside just add 5 to the number of inside dots to find the area. I then went on to look at shapes with 24 dots on the outside. With these geoboard shapes, add 11 to the number of inside dots to get the area. I then looked at several other geoboard shapes and my chart looked like this:

3 out	*add 5 to inside*
6 out	*add 2*
12 out	*add 5*
24 out	*add 11*

I then started to see if I could expand my chart to all numbers, not just multiples of 3. In the end I came up with this: (out dots = T, in dots = C)

$$.5 \times (T-2) + C$$

Habits of Learning

In the examples students observe, question, and challenge the material of mathematics. They are making sense by making meaning, and discovering for themselves what it means to do mathematics. For many students the notion that mathematics is something that people *do*, not something that comes from the sky, is a surprising discovery. That they themselves can do mathematics is even more remarkable news.

This year a sixth grader wrote:

I think mathematics is a kind of system that was invented to make life easier. You take what you have, you calculate it in some way and then you get something else. It might be what you had or what you're going to get.

In my opinion to use math a person needs to know two things. Those two things are the ability to do the calculations of math, but also know what the calculations mean.

The student work included in this book shows how writing helps learners construct their understanding of mathematics. I believe that writing—the practice of which involves habits of the hand—encourages students to develop habits of the mind and eventually habits of the heart. Cultivating hands, hearts, and minds is good work for teachers, and for learners.

Appendix

You have been invited to the emperor's banquet. The emperor is a rather strange host. Instead of sitting with his guests at his large round dining table, he walks around the table pouring oats on the head of every other person. He continues this process, pouring oats on the head of everyone who has not had oats until there is only one person left. The question is, where should you sit if you do not want oats poured on your head?

If you are the only guest you have no problem for the emperor will not pour oats on your head. If there are two guests then you should head for seat number two. If there are three guests the emperor will pour oats on the heads of the people sitting in seats numbered one and three, so you should sit in seat number two. If there are four guests, however, the emperor will pour oats on the head of the person sitting in seat number one, skip number two, pour oats on number three, skip number four, and pour oats on two. Therefore you should choose seat four.

As some of the students point out in Chapter Five, making a list helps reveal an interesting pattern:

Number of people	Seat to choose	
1	1	2^0
2	2	2^1
3	2	
4	4	2^2

Number of people	Seat to choose	
5	2	
6	4	
7	6	
8	8	2^3
9	2	
10	4	
11	6	
12	8	
13	10	
14	12	
15	14	
16	16	2^4

The solution seems related to powers of two. One way to proceed when you arrive at the banquet is to count the number of guests, subtract from that number the highest power of two that is less than the number, double the result, and choose that seat. For example, if there are thirty-six guests, subtract thirty-two (2^5) from thirty-six, which leaves four; four times two equals eight. That's your seat. Try it.

Endnotes

Chapter One

1. My understanding of the writing process has been enhanced by reading the work of Ann Berthoff, James Britton, Peter Elbow, Janet Emig, Toby Fulwiler, Susan Lytle, Ken Macrorie, and Peter Stillman. See bibliography for suggestions.

Chapter Five

1. The mathematician Henry Pollack was director of research at Bell Labs. Now retired, he continues to be deeply involved in the movement for change in mathematics education. He used the phrase "biography of the numbers" in a discussion about identifying students who succeed in secondary mathematics.

Chapter Seven

1. The open-ended questions and scoring rubric are described in *Assessment Alternatives in Mathematics*, prepared by the EQUALS staff and the Assessment Committee of the California Mathematics Council.

Bibliography

American Association for the Advancement of Science. 1989. *Science for All Americans, Project 2061.* Washington, D.C.

Barnes, Douglas. 1979. *From Communication to Curriculum.* New York: Penguin Books.

Barr, Mary, Pat D'Arcy, and Mary K. Healy. 1982. *What's Going On?* Portsmouth, N.H.: Boynton/Cook.

Bell, Elizabeth S., and Ronald N. Bell. 1985. "Writing and Mathematical Problem Solving: Arguments in Favor of Synthesis." *School Science and Mathematics* 85(March): 210–21.

Berthoff, Ann. 1982. *Forming/Thinking/Writing: The Composing Imagination.* Portsmouth, N.H.: Boynton/Cook.

———. 1984. *Reclaiming the Imagination.* Portsmouth, N.H.: Boynton/Cook.

Britton, James. 1970. *Language and Learning.* New York: Penguin Books.

———. 1982. *Prospect and Retrospect: Selected Essays.* Edited by Gordon M. Pradle. Portsmouth, N.H.: Boynton/Cook.

Brown, Stephen I., and Marion Walter. 1983. *The Art of Problem Posing.* Philadelphia: The Franklin Institute Press.

Buerk, Dorothy. 1982. "An Experience with Some Able Women Who Avoid Mathematics." *For the Learning of Mathematics* (Canada) 3(2):19–24.

Burton, G. M. 1988. "Helping Your Students Make Sense out of Math." *Learning,* January, 31–36.

Burton, Leone. 1988. *Thinking Things Through.* Cambridge, Mass.: Basil Blackwell.

Calkins, Lucy McCormick. 1986. *The Art of Teaching Writing.* Portsmouth, N.H.: Boynton/Cook.

Camp, Gerald, ed. 1984. *Teaching Writing: Essays from the Bay Area Writing Project.* Portsmouth, N.H.: Boynton/Cook.

Crosswhite, F. Joe, John Dossey, and Shirley Frye. 1989. "NCTM Standards for School Mathematics: Visions for Implementation." *Mathematics Teacher* 82(November): 664–71.

Davison, David M., and Daniel L. Pearce. 1988. "Using Writing Activities to Reinforce Mathematics Instruction." *Arithmetic Teacher* 35:42–45.

Elbow, Peter. 1973. *Writing Without Teachers.* New York: Oxford University Press.

Emig, Janet. 1983. *The Web of Meaning.* Portsmouth, N.H.: Boynton/Cook.

Evans, Christine Sebray. 1984. "Writing to Learn in Math." *Language Arts* 51(8):828–35.

Fulwiler, Toby. 1982. "Writing: An Act of Cognition." In *Teaching Writing in All Disciplines. See* Griffin 1982.

———. 1986. "The Argument for Writing Across the Curriculum." In *Writing Across the Disciplines,* edited by Art Young and Toby Fulwiler. Portsmouth, N.H.: Boynton/Cook.

———. 1987. *The Journal Book.* Portsmouth, N.H.: Boynton/Cook.

Fulwiler, Toby, and Art Young, eds. 1982. *Language Connections: Writing and Reading Across the Curriculum.* Urbana, Ill.: National Council of Teachers of English.

Geeslin, William. 1977. "Using Writing About Mathematics as a Teaching Technique." *Mathematics Teacher* 70 (February):112–15.

Gere, Ann Ruggles, ed. 1985. *Roots in the Sawdust: Writing to Learn Across the Disciplines.* Urbana Ill.: National Council of Teachers of English.

Griffin, C. Williams, ed. 1982. *Teaching Writing in All Disciplines*. New Directions for Teaching and Learning, edited by Kenneth E. Eble and John Noonen, no. 12. San Francisco: Jossey-Bass.

Grumbacher, Judy. 1985. "Writing to Learn Physics." In *Research in Writing: Reports from a Teacher-Researcher Seminar*. Fairfax, Vir.: Northern Virginia Writing Project.

Hays, Janice, et al., eds. 1983. *The Writer's Mind: Writing as a Mode of Thinking*. Urbana, Ill.: National Council of Teachers of English.

Johnson, Marvin L. 1983. "Writing in Mathematics Classes: A Valuable Tool for Learning." *Mathematics Teacher 76* (February):117–19.

Kasner, Edward, and James R. Newman. 1989. *Mathematics and the Imagination*. Redmond, Wash.: Microsoft, Tempus Books.

Kennedy, Bill. 1985. "Writing Letters to Learn Math." *Learning*, February, 59–61.

Kirkpatrick, Larry D., and Adele S. Pigttendrigh. 1984. "A Writing Teacher in the Physics Classroom." *The Physics Teacher*, March, 159–64.

LeGere, Adele. 1991. "Collaboration and Writing in the Mathematics Classroom." *Mathematics Teacher* 84(March):166–71.

McIntosh, Margaret E. 1991. "No Time for Writing in Your Class?" *Mathematics Teacher* 84(September):423–33.

Macrorie, Ken. 1988. The I-Search Paper. Portsmouth, N.H.: Boynton/Cook.

Martin, Nancy. 1984. *Writing Across the Curriculum Pamphlets: A Selection from the Schools Council and London University Institute of Education Joint Writing Across the Curriculum Project*. Portsmouth, N.H.: Boynton/Cook.

———, ed. 1976. *Writing Across the Curriculum*. Portsmouth, N.H.: Boynton/Cook.

Martin, Nancy, Pat D'Arcy, Bryan Newton, and Robert Parker. [1976] 1984. *Writing and Learning Across the Curriculum 11-16*. [London: Ward Lock Educational] Portsmouth, N.H.: Boynton/Cook.

Mathematical Sciences Education Board. National Research Council. 1990. *Reshaping School Mathematics: A Framework for Curriculum.* Washington, D.C.: National Academy Press.

Mayher, John S., Nancy Lester, and Gordon Pradl. 1983. *Learning to Write/Writing to Learn.* Portsmouth, N.H.: Boynton/Cook.

Mett, Coreen L. 1987. "Writing as a Learning Device in Calculus." *Mathematics Teacher* 80(October):534–37.

Miller, Loretta Diane. 1991. "Writing to Learn Mathematics." *Mathematics Teacher* 84(October):516–21.

Moffet, James. 1981. *Active Voice: A Writing Program Across the Curriculum.* Portsmouth, N.H.: Boynton/Cook.

Murray, Donald M. 1982. *Learning by Teaching: Selected Articles on Writing and Teaching.* Portsmouth, N.H.: Heinemann.

Myers, John W. 1984. *Writing to Learn Across the Curriculum.* Bloomington, Ind.: Phi Delta Kappa Educational Foundation.

Nahrgang, Cynthia L., and Bruce T. Petersen. 1986. "Using Writing to Learn Mathematics." *Mathematics Teacher* 79 (September):461–65.

National Council of Teachers of Mathematics. 1989. *Curriculum and Evaluation Standards for School Mathematics.* Reston, Vir.

National Research Council. 1989. *Everybody Counts: A Report on the Future of Mathematics Education.* Washington, D.C.: National Academy Press.

Orr, Eleanor Wilson. 1987. *Twice As Less.* New York: W. W. Norton.

Polanyi, Michael. 1964. Personal Knowledge. New York: HarperCollins, Harper Torchbooks.

Resnick, Lauren. 1987. *Education and Learning to Think.* Committee on Mathematics, Science, and Technology Education. NRC. Washington, D.C.: National Academy Press.

Salem, Judith. 1982. "Using Writing in Teaching Mathematics." In *What's Going On? See* Barr 1982.

Savage, Wendy. 1981. Letter to the Editor. *Mathematics Teaching* 94(March):7.

Silver, Edward A., Jeremy Kilpatrick, and Beth Schlesinger. 1991. *Thinking Through Mathematics: Fostering Inquiry and Communication in Mathematics Classrooms.* New York: The College Board.

Steen, Lynn Arthur, ed. 1990. *On the Shoulders of Giants: New Approaches to Numeracy.* Mathematical Sciences Education Board. NRC. Washington, D.C.: National Academy Press.

Stempien, M., and Raffaella Borasi. 1985. "Students' Writing in Mathematics: Some Ideas and Experiences. *For the Learning of Mathematics* (Canada) 5(3):14–17.

Stenmark, Jean Kerr. 1989. *Assessment Alternatives in Mathematics: An Overview of Assessment Techniques that Promote Learning.* Berkeley, Calif.: Lawrence Hall of Science.

Stillman, Peter. 1984 *Writing Your Way.* Portsmouth, N.H.: Boynton/Cook.

Tchudi, Stephen, and Margie Huerta. 1983. *Teaching Writing in the Content Areas.* Washington, D.C.: National Education Association.

Tchudi, Stephen, and Joanne Yates. 1983. *Teaching Writing in the Content Areas: Senior High School.* Washington, D.C.: National Education Association.

Torbe, Mike, and Peter Medway. 1981. *The Climate for Learning.* Portsmouth, N.H.: Heinemann.

Torbe, Mike, et al. 1982. *Mathematics.* Language, Teaching and Learning, no. 6. London: Ward Lock Educational.

Van den Brink, J. "Children as Arithmetic Authors." *For the Learning of Mathematics* (Canada) 7(2):44–47.

Watson, Margaret. 1980. "Writing Has a Place in a Mathematics Class." *Mathematics Teacher* 73(October):518–19.

Young, Art, and Toby Fulwiler, eds. 1986. *Writing Across the Disciplines.* Portsmouth, N.H.: Boynton/Cook.

Zinsser, William. 1980. *On Writing Well.* New York: HarperCollins.

———. 1988. *Writing to Learn.* New York: HarperCollins.